STORMY VICTORY
The Story of TCHAIKOVSKY

Books by
Claire Lee Purdy

STORMY VICTORY
The Story of Tchaikovsky

SONG OF THE NORTH
The Story of Edvard Grieg

HE HEARD AMERICA SING
The Story of Stephen Foster

ANTONIN DVORAK
Composer from Bohemia

GILBERT AND SULLIVAN
Masters of Mirth and Melody

VICTOR HERBERT
American Music-Master

STORMY VICTORY

BY CLAIRE LEE PURDY

The story of

TCHAIKOVSKY

with decorations

BY VERA BOCK

MUSIC DRAWINGS BY RUDOLF W. KOHL

JULIAN MESSNER
NEW YORK

PUBLISHED BY JULIAN MESSNER

DIVISION OF POCKET BOOKS, INC.

8 WEST 40 STREET, NEW YORK 10018

© COPYRIGHT 1942 BY POCKET BOOKS, INC.

TWELFTH PRINTING, 1966

232081

PRINTED IN THE UNITED STATES OF AMERICA

I made the decorations in this book in tribute to the memory of Tchaikovsky. I dedicate them to my mother who knew him, who, in the early days of her career as a pianist, played when Tchaikovsky conducted, and who, speaking of him, made me know him too.

V. B.

Contents

(To set the mood and suggest the theme of the narrative to come, a few measures of the emotional, beautifully descriptive folk-songs of Russia precede each chapter. The names of these songs appear below.)

Prelude

1 9 4 2

Strong, nervous fingers, pianist's fingers. Hands white under the glaring lights. Whiter than the ivories of the keyboard. A great artist is recording Tchaikovsky's Piano Concerto in B flat minor. Vigorous, triumphant chords. The orchestra takes up the strange melody. It is like a challenge now. Defiant. What is it saying, asserting?

1 8 9 1

Carnegie Hall. The architect stands on the stage. In the midst of his little speech he looks up. Rows upon rows of people in balconies hanging by threads over rows and rows of other people. Fear grips him! The steel in this building. Will it carry the load? Has it been figured correctly? Suppose— He rushes out to figure the stresses once more. It is good. There has been no mistake.

On the stage Walter Damrosch has stepped down from the conductor's podium and a slender, white-haired man is taking his place. It is Peter Ilich Tchaikovsky come all the way from Russia to conduct his own works at the opening of New York's great music hall. He raises the baton. The audience stirs at the opening bars of the music. *Marche solennelle.* What is this man saying in his music? Something he could not say in words? Something he dared not say in the land of the Tsars?

1 8 9 3

The late evening sun makes an amber light on the pages of the music lying on a table in an upstairs bedroom. No one is at home. The composer is out walking bareheaded on the steppe. He is singing as he goes. By its four corners he carries a handkerchief into which he has put fat mushrooms found in the wood. This is the Hermit of Klin.

Alexis, his servant, scolds him a little when he returns, takes the mushrooms, and goes off to tell the cook that the master has returned and will want his supper. Peter Ilich Tchaikovsky sits down at the piano in his living room, plays the music which is written on the pages on his table. No need to read the notes. They are out of his own head. The *Pathétique.* He plays the somber opening chords of his last symphony. What sort of music is this? Prometheus bound, crying curses? Challenge in the midst of agony? What is this man trying to say? Who is he, anyway? What is his story?

Should you like to learn it? It goes back to the days before Norse Rurik and Genghis Khan, when the Slavs sang their melancholy songs in the valleys of Russia.

1 8 4 0

It begins with the birth of a son to the Mining Inspector for the Tsar in the town of Votkinsk on the borders of Asia, where the hunters of the Ural Mountains track down the wolf howling his savage hunger to the moon.

Should you like to hear a strange tale? Listen!

Yule-tide wakes, Yule-tide breaks, Wom-an, give me eggs and cakes.

1

"Zdravstvuitye!" This mouth-filling, room-filling Russian "How do you do?" came booming from the entrance hall of the Tchaikovsky home.

"It's Blinof!" The children shouted in chorus and swarmed down the stairs to greet their Russian tutor. They surrounded the good-natured young man and hindered more than they helped him to take off his heavy fur-lined coat. Blinof made a huge but somehow pleasant racket as he beat the dry snow from his fur cap and knocked some of the ice from his boots.

"Hurry, Blinof! Father and mother are almost ready to show us the tree." Handsome young Nicholas, eldest son of the household by virtue of his six years of experience of earthly joys and sorrows, tugged at the tutor's arm.

"I was afraid you had forgotten." Shy Peter Ilich, two years younger than his brother, looked up at Blinof with that charming smile that made him, despite his perpetually tousled hair and untidy linen, the most attractive member of the household.

"Forget? How you talk, Petrushka! Forget to come to see your Christmas tree?" Blinof stooped and lifted young Peter to a position astride his ample neck, and Peter clasped his arms around the young man's throat affectionately and kissed him three times on the top of his head.

"And how is my little sweetheart, who is going to marry me when she is old enough to wind her braids around her head and I have a snow-white beard to tuck into my blouse?" Blinof smiled down at laughing-eyed Lidia, the boys' young cousin, who had come to live with the Tchaikovskys when her mother died.

Lidia's pink cheeks grew crimson at the tutor's jest. She was older than Nicholas and was beginning to feel that she should not be chaffed and teased any more as mere children are.

Grabbing Lidia and Nicholas by the hand and carrying Peter astride his strong shoulders, Blinof mounted the stairs. He sang a gay Russian folk-song that goes like this:

Postilion's Song

On the sturdy wooden bridge,
    Strutting gaily up and down
Goes a bold and handsome fellow,
    He's the post-man of the town.

See his stylish coat of blue;
    See his coat-tails swinging gay!
See his ruffled shirt of linen
    And his waistcoat puffed and gray!

And he flourishes his stick
    As he swaggers to and fro.
What a gallant, what a dandy,
    What a lady-killing beau!

Allegretto

And his neck - er - chief so red, like a pop - py in the dew; from his pock - et sticks an - oth - er of a bright I - ta - lian blue.

At the top of the stairs a smiling group waited for Blinof and the children. Father Ilya Tchaikovsky, kindly and cheerful, was beaming and nodding his approval. Mother Alexandra, always more reserved but never less kind or thoughtful than her husband, smiled her greeting. Clasping her mother's hand tightly and staring with wondering baby eyes at Blinof and her brothers was two-year-old Alexandra, called Sasha for short. The children's great-aunt Valzeva stood beside the *babushka* (grandmother) of the household, whose wrinkled face was creased further with her happy smiles. Standing a little apart from the family group was Mademoiselle Fanny Dürbach, the French governess who had joined the Tchaikovsky household in the fall to teach Nicholas and Lidia French, German, and history. Fanny Dürbach's sensitive young face and expressive eyes had immediately won for her a lasting place in the hearts of the Tchaikovsky family, who treated her like a well-loved younger sister.

There was a shower of good Russian greetings. "Dobroye vecher" (Good evening), and "Kak pozhivayetye" (How are you?), and of course "Zdravstvuitye" (How do you do?).

"But where is my little pigeon?" Blinof asked, looking about for the crib and the baby of the house, eight-months-old Hippolite.

"Fast asleep upstairs," Mother Tchaikovsky told him. "Christmas will not be for him until next year."

This hearty Christmas scene was taking place in the small mining town of Votkinsk, which lies on the Kama River in the foothills of the Ural Mountains. The fir-clad slopes of the Urals, which are very old and so are worn down to smooth, rolling, not very high mountains, without forbidding cliffs or sky-piercing peaks, form a sort of wall between Europe and Asia. It was across this wall that the "Golden Horde" of the Tatar Khans of Mongolia poured centuries ago—the Golden Horde who derived their name from the fact that Batu, powerful and wealthy Khan, had a golden tent set up on the banks of the Volga. They subdued the peaceful Slavic peoples of the Russian steppes (plains), bent the proud descendants of the northern Varangian princes to their will, mixed their blood with that of the conquered, and so formed a race of people with strange poetry and music in them, a people strong and patient, a people of mirth and melancholy, of tumultuous destiny.

It was Christmas Eve in the year 1844 in the land of the Russian Bear. Everywhere in this huge land—from the arctic wastes of Siberia to the citrus groves in the southern province of Georgia, from beyond Votkinsk and the Urals to the east, to the Tsar's capital city of St. Petersburg (modern Leningrad) on the Baltic, which is Russia's European window—the deep muffling snows of the severe Russian winter covered the black soil.

Russia was not a country but a world, and in the nineteenth century a strangely aloof world. An earthquake was shaking the rest of the European nations—the Industrial Revolution, which opened the floodgates to invention. Machines issued forth in a torrent which was to sweep away forever the ancient handcraft methods of producing goods, and eventu-

ally to raise mankind above the age-old slavery of working from dawn to dark for the bare essentials of life.

Some doubted and distrusted the machines, but there was no way to stop the flood which in the process of freeing men overwhelmed many in a sea of unemployment, depression, insecurity, wage slavery, and war. Like some Frankenstein monster, the machine age ran berserk, and only a few saw and believed that it would someday be controlled and directed for man's happiness.

Machines, hundreds of machines! By 1840, people were familiar with the names of the textile inventions: Kay's "flying shuttle," Hargreaves' "spinning jenny," Arkwright's "water-frame," Crompton's "spinning mule," Cartwright's "power loom," Whitney's "cotton gin."

The steam engine was invented. Then steam was applied to transport: Fulton built a successful steamboat in 1807; Stephenson demonstrated his rail locomotive in 1825.

Electricity was captured and put to work, and Morse used this new slave when he invented the telegraph in 1837.

Hoes and sickles and crooked-stick plows were laid aside when McCormick invented the reaper in 1834, and quickly followed this invention with steam-driven plows and cultivators.

Ericsson invented the screw propeller in 1836. Goodyear learned how to vulcanize rubber in 1844. Daguerre invented photography in 1839.

Cheap methods for producing iron in large quantities were being developed. This led to the making of lathes, grinders, milling cutters for working metals. These were the machines which were the breeders of machines. The flood expanded, rose higher and higher, swept before it the manufacturing, farming, and transport methods of the Middle Ages.

Only the enormous land of Russia resisted the flood. There the serf—the farm slave—tilled the land with tools as primitive as those used in Biblical times. There the peasant brought his produce to market in wooden carts with squealing wheels, and the roads he traveled were quagmires in spring and frozen ruts in fall. Volga boatmen walked the towpath, making themselves beasts of burden to pull heavy barges upriver.

Who could foretell that in less than a hundred years the great Russian people would stir, yawn, stretch, wake up, rise from its sleeping, stride out like some giant of old, stride out to the dam and open the gates to progress, to the machines which would in twenty years sweep aside the ignorance of a hundred centuries? In 1840, Russia huddled around brick ovens during the cold winters, turned its back on the machines, and slept.

In the Tsar's palace, in the pretentious three-story homes of the rich *boyars* (noblemen), in the comfortable homes of government officials like Ilya Tchaikovsky, even in the miserable huts of the peasant serfs, lights burned before the sacred *ikons* (pictures of the saints of the Greek Catholic Church). The wealthy and moderately wealthy sat down to tables loaded with rich Christmas meats and imported wines. The poor sat down to black rye bread and cabbage soup. All sang the songs and told the tales which are free to all, rich and poor alike.

It was a miserable beggar indeed—some shivering blind creature, perhaps, or homeless waif—who did not have a little something with which to cheer himself on Christmas Eve; but truth to tell, there were too many such outcasts. Even as the cheerful songs were sung, the great Russian Bear stirred uneasily, aware that on his back he carried too many bare huts, too few comfortable homes.

But anyway it was Christmas Eve. "Nichevo!" (What does it matter!) Uneasily the *muzhik*, the well-to-do peasant, shrugged his shoulders, glancing sidelong at his ragged serf neighbors kneeling in the village church. "Nichevo!" Reckless young noblemen tossed off glasses of the fiery vodka, mind-and-conscience-killing drink of old Russia. *What does it matter? Let us celebrate as best we may, while we may.*

In many a home some old grandmother gathered the children around her chair and told them the traditional Christmas tales. Grandmothers in rustling black silks and fine lace fichus. Grandmothers in coarse homespun. Homes brilliantly lighted with oil lamps and wax candles. One-room huts foul with the odor of unwashed bodies, fetid with the breathing of too many people in air renewed only by the blast that entered when the outer door was opened to let someone out or in.

Russia was a land of black and white contrasts, a sprawling land stretching to vast horizons, presenting an ever-changing face, like that of some magnificent old tragedian. In the great cities of St. Petersburg and Moscow, the bronze bells of the Peter-Paul Cathedral, Ivan the Great's Bell Tower, St. Basil's Church, and scores of other cathedrals, churches, and monasteries made a mighty din. In the frozen streets, sleighs were drawn briskly along by teams of horses hitched *troika* fashion, the center or shaft horse with the high *duga* (collar), the outer horses on loose reins. The spirited trotting of the troika teams made a pleasant background for the musical clamor of little silver harness bells. Lights from fine hotels and restaurants, where smartly uniformed officers danced with girls wearing frocks from Paris, streamed out to light the walks outside. Along broad boulevards, oil lamps on ornamental posts twinkled like stars in the cold night.

On the wind-swept steppes, peasant huts huddled together in the drifted snow as if they sought to warm each other. Windows were sealed tight against the cold, so that the poor light from burning rushes and crude lamps and the brief flare of wood fire when stove doors were opened to receive added fuel did not reach the road and streets. Hamlets and villages were lighted only by the moon and stars, which seemed to have cast millions of precious glittering diamonds on the snowfields stretching endlessly to the vast horizons.

Far to the east, the ancient city of Nizhni-Novgorod lay like some hibernating bear, slumbering and waiting for summer and the time of its great fair, when Tatar and Byzantine merchants would meet buyers from northern Europe to exchange tea and furs and tallow and silks and spices and rugs for gold or for the manufactured goods from Manchester and Sheffield, Hamburg and Paris and Doorn. Here it was, too, that magnificent "Mother Volga," largest river of Europe, rested silent for many months under her ice shroud.

And farther still to the east even than Nizhni-Novgorod, the frozen Kama River, tributary to the Volga, laid a frigid crystal ribbon across snow-drifted valleys. Along this icebound river straggled the huts and government buildings of the mining town of Votkinsk.

Under the pines of the hills behind Votkinsk the snow lay deep. All the little creatures of the forest slept their winter's sleep in snug earthen burrows, and the great brown bears had forgotten to be fierce, for the strange drowsiness of the hibernating season was upon them. Only the gaunt Russian wolf roamed forest and steppe, howling his hungry protest to the moon.

In the largest house in Votkinsk—the home of the Tsar's Inspector of Mines, Ilya Tchaikovsky—the lamps burned brightly and the huge porcelain-and-tile stoves poured warmth into the large rooms. On the ground floor were the kitchens and servants' quarters, an arrangement common to all well-to-do households. A large staff of servants—peasant boys and girls from the neighboring farms—laughed and sang around their samovar (tea urn) in celebration of Christmas. On the third floor, in his little room under the roof, baby Hippolite slept blissfully unaware of the excitement in other parts of the house. On the second floor, where the family had their living-rooms, Lidia's Uncle Ilya, who was the father of Nicholas, Peter, Hippolite, and Sasha, flung open the dining-room doors and shouted with laughter to see how the children tumbled over their own feet to get to the tree.

Mother Alexandra Tchaikovsky moved quickly to keep Sasha from rushing right in among the presents under the tree. Aunt Valzeva and Fanny Dürbach helped the old *matushka* (mother) walk to her warm corner near the stove. Blinof sat on the floor with the children around him to wait for Father Ilya to hand out the gifts.

Very soon the mysterious packages were a mystery no longer. Nicholas hugged his gift of shining skates close to him. Peter hopped up and down to try out his new red-leather boots. Lidia's cheeks were pink and her eyes sparkling when she lifted a dainty French frock and schoolgirl's apron from a pretty box. Mother and Father and Grandmother, Blinof and Fanny Dürbach, exclaimed and chuckled over their own presents.

In the midst of the *oh*-ing and *ah*-ing, in came the girls from the kitchen. They set the huge family samovar, glasses, and spoons on the table, along with platters of holiday cakes. The peasant girls in their wide gathered dresses and shapeless shoes were invited to stay a while and look at the gifts. There was wistfulness in their eyes as they looked at Lidia's frock from Paris. Stolid faces broke into wide grins when Father Ilya brought a large box from under the tree. It was filled with small gifts for the kitchen staff, and the girls hurried below to open it with the others.

These girls were part of the staff provided by the government for the Inspector of Mines. They belonged to the house in much the same way that the farm serfs belonged to the land, passing from one master to another as the years went by.

The children's chatter was like the twittering of swallows in the summer vines. Honey and nut cakes and the Christmas gingerbread called *pryanik* disappeared from the platters as if they had been piles of snow under a warm spring sun. Mother drew water from the samovar into tall glasses into which she had poured a little of the strong tea steeping in a pot at the top of the huge copper urn.

Mademoiselle Fanny Dürbach drew back into the shadows of a window alcove and studied the vivacious Russian family, those intelligent, sympathetic eyes of hers missing no detail. She was thinking how amazing it was that she, a French girl with roots also in German soil, should be sitting in a warm living-room hundreds of miles from the Europe she knew. How she had dreaded, just two months before, the thought of leaving St. Petersburg, where she made her living as a tutor of French, to go into the desolate mining region! It was only because gentle, kindly Mother Alexandra herself had been in the city to talk over details that Fanny had found the courage. It had been a three-week journey by post coach and by river boat from St. Petersburg to Votkinsk. Small wonder that she had had misgivings about going so far to become part of a household strange to her. Years later she recalled the end of that journey:

"The nearer we drew to the journey's end, the more restless and anxious I became. On our arrival, a single moment sufficed to dispel all my fears. A number of people came out to meet us, and in the general greeting and embracing it was difficult to distinguish relatives from servants. All fraternized in the sincerity of their joy. The head of the family kissed me without ceremony, as though I had been his daughter. It seemed less like a first arrival than a return home."

Fanny's dreaming was interrupted by a commotion which centered around Mother Alexandra's chair.

"Do please play for us!" the children begged.

"The riddle song. We want to learn our fortunes!" Lidia and Nicholas urged the laughing mother of the family toward the door into the music-room.

Seated at the piano, Mother Alexandra called over her shoulder, "Pierre!" The children's mother was as much French as Russian and often used this French form of Peter Ilich's name. "Hurry down to the kitchen and get a bowl. The rest choose your trinkets. Let us not keep the future waiting!"

This was a game as old as the steppes of Russia. Each child put some personal belonging into the bowl on the table. Father Ilya was chosen to draw the trinkets out one by one while the children sang this song to their mother's accompaniment:

RIDDLE SONG

Now a ring of gold do I hide, do I hide;
Now a silver dish do I hide, do I hide;
Find the silver, find the gold,
Guess the riddle I have told!

Now a string of pearls do I hide, do I hide;
Now a crystal cup do I hide, do I hide;
Find the crystal, find the pearl,
Guess the riddle, pretty girl!

As each trinket was drawn from the dish, the piano-playing
and singing would stop instantly. The word at which the
song was chopped off was supposed to give the owner of the
article drawn from the dish some clue as to his future work
or love or general happiness and destiny.

"Now a golden pin do I hide, do I hide," sang the children; "Now an ivory—"

"My locket!" squealed Lidia. "But what does 'ivory'
mean?"

"No doubt it means that you will be going to India and
ride on an elephant," teased her uncle.

"Or live in an ivory tower, like the princess in the fairy
tale," suggested Fanny Dürbach.

The song had begun again:

"Find the pin and find the fan," sang the children ex-
citedly, more than half believing in their absurd "magic";
"Guess the riddle—"

The trinket drawn out at this point was a toy belonging to Peter Ilich, who stood watching his mother's hands as they flew across the keys of the piano.

"The riddle!" shouted Nicholas. "What does that mean?" Fanny Dürbach, who had been watching the rapt expression on Peter's face while he listened to the music, thought to herself:

"Guess the riddle—if you can! Could it be music?" The governess frowned at the thought. She had grown to be fond of little "Pierre." And she knew Russia of that day. Musicians had an incredibly difficult time in a land where the great majority of the people could not have afforded to attend a concert even if they had not already been denied the opportunities for education and culture necessary to the enjoyment of good music. Men and women who made music their profession and who were dependent for their living on that profession had to rely on the meager fees from teaching, on the fickle patronage of the wealthy.

If they were composers, their lot was even worse; for most Russians turned up their noses at native talent, preferring Italian opera and French and German concert music. In any case, fees from performances or publication of musical works were ridiculously small.

"Non, non, non!" Fanny's eyes flashed. "We must discourage this tendency. Music shall not be for our Pierre!"

"Fanny! Did you know that you were talking to yourself? And you said something about Pierre. Tell me what it was while he is claiming his toy from the bowl."

The governess flushed. "It was nothing, Madame. A foolish fancy. An intuition, a feeling that music is a dangerous companion for Pierre."

"Dangerous?" Mother looked keenly at the French girl.

"He has a talent for it," explained Fanny simply.

"I see. And you think this talent must be discouraged? Perhaps you are right. Yes, I am sure you are."

"If Madame will agree, I shall encourage him to turn his talent to poetry. Even at his age he shows an aptitude for it. He is most gifted, our Pierre. Lidia and Nicholas and I call him 'the little Pushkin'—just among ourselves, of course."

"As you think best, Fanny." And so it was decided without consulting Peter Ilich that his artistic talents were to be turned toward poetry and away from music. Peter, always docile and eager to please those about him, earnestly filled his notebooks with poetic scribblings for years to come. He kept his yearnings toward music mostly to himself.

When all the trinkets from the bowl had been drawn out, Mother gathered her young brood around her. Sleepy goodnights were said to Father and Grandmother, Blinof and Fanny Dürbach. Soon the children were snuggled in their warm beds.

The snow had stopped falling, and the moon's bright disc gleamed on the pine tree outside Peter Ilich's window. From across the white wastes came the sound of men's voices singing. The Cossacks at the barracks below the house were making merry with Christmas meats and wine.

Peter listened, as he always did, with deep attention. Though foolish, well-meaning Fanny Dürbach and his parents might, out of their love for him, try to keep him from music, they had no way of keeping music from him. Songs of the reapers in the fields in summer, of the serf miners trudging homeward in the autumn twilight, songs of the Cossacks in the frosty night—these impressions of Peter's youth stayed with him all the days of his life. Something of all this went into such songs as "The Tapers Were Flashing," which grown-up Peter Ilich Tchaikovsky, the composer, wrote to words of the great Russian writer Tolstoi.

What so vast, what so green as the Rus-sian plain?

2

*C*hristmas Day brought with it such a snow storm as even the old *matushka*, the children's grandmother, could not remember having experienced. The air was so thick with the large feathery flakes that try as he might, with his nose pressed against one of the windows, young Peter Ilich could not see as far as the barracks where the Cossacks bivouacked. Even the fence and gate beside the garden path were merely formless shadows looming up vaguely beyond the wall of white.

The excitement of Christmas Eve had left the children listless and somewhat bored. All the new toys had been played with, the new boots and dresses and blouses tried on. In short, there was nothing to do.

Great-aunt Valzeva was tired and cross. Father Ilya had braved the storm in high boots and long fur coat, to pay a visit to a sick friend. Mother was busy with her youngest children, Sasha and Hippolite. Mademoiselle Dürbach was writing letters. Grandmother dozed by the fire in her room. Christmas Day was decidedly not Christmas Eve.

"It wouldn't be so bad," said Lidia, "if we could go out and play in the snow, but Aunt Sasha says that with the snow falling so thick we could easily get lost in our own yard and might even wander out beyond to the hills before we knew it."

There was a shiver from Nicholas, whose pet name was Kolya. "Then we'd be like the girl who met the Frost King," he said.

The tale Nicholas spoke of was one as old surely as the hills behind Votkinsk. At any rate, it was very old, and specially beloved of those who knew what it meant to lack proper clothes and bedding. It had taken form in bare, dreary rooms where peasant families lived.

"I think Osip is in the kitchen," said Nicholas, brightening up considerably at the thought. "Let's get him to tell us a story." Osip was one of the house servants at Votkinsk, a young serf who had lived his boyhood in a mean thatched hut, where the family huddled around the huge brick stove and dipped their wooden spoons into a common bowl of cabbage soup, made with a little meat only in honor of special holidays like Christmas.

"Oh, Kolya! You know that Osip knows only one story," grumbled Lidia. "At least it's the only one you can get him to tell. And we know by heart that tale about the Ox, the Ram, the Pig, and the Goose!"

"I don't know it by heart yet," announced Peter so unexpectedly that Lidia and Nicholas laughed.

"Come on then, Petia. We'll find Osip." Nicholas ran toward the stairs, Peter at his heels. Lidia with less enthusiasm followed.

They found Osip just dropping the armload of wood he had been carrying in from a box outside the kitchen door. He was a tall, thin, gangling youth, with a shock of butter-colored hair and a nose that stuck straight out like a pump handle. He grinned when he saw the children, for he knew right well what they came for.

"Are you busy, Osip?" asked Nicholas.

"*Da* [Yes]." Osip was in a mood for teasing.

The children looked disappointed. "We wanted you to tell us a story," explained Peter. "Can't you stop bringing in wood for just a little while?"

"*Niet* [No]!"

"Oh, Osip!" exploded Lidia, who was not to be taken in with all this nonsense. "You *can* stop. And if you don't tell us a story, we shall all just die of boredom and nothing to do!"

"You might help me bring in the wood," suggested Osip slyly. "Nothing like work to kill that feeling."

"Osip! Mind what you say," growled the cook, a fat peasant woman who had just come in from the pantry. "Less than that would have brought the lash down on your shoulders if the master we had before these children's father came had heard you!"

Peter was looking distressed. "Nobody is lashed in this house," he said with a certain grown-up dignity that made people forget that he was hardly more than a baby, not yet five years old. "Please, Osip, tell us a story."

"Tell it." The old cook nodded her head. "I will make some tea for us while you weave your fancies."

Osip hunched his angular frame into a comfortable chair near the stove, and the children drew up stools and sat at his feet. The peasant lad half-closed his eyes when he talked, and his oddly compelling voice borrowed enough of the music of the old *skazka* (folk tale) to make pleasing poetry of the story of the Ox, the Ram, the Pig, and the Goose.

"They were a very restless, discontented people, my little pigeons." Thus Osip explained the urge which sent the four animals traveling in search of a land where winter could not reach them. "Yes, they were restless, and they were foolish enough to believe what they had not seen with their own eyes, tasted with their own tongues, heard with their own ears. Yes, my little pigeons, they believed the tale of a blind beggar at the fair of Nizhni-Novgorod. He sang them a song about a land of orange trees and flowers, where winter snows never fell, and they believed this song. Now we know better. There is no land where the Frost King does not dwell."

"But, Osip, there is!" Peter interrupted eagerly. "Mademoiselle Dürbach has told us many times about Italy, and our own country to the south. Orange trees grow there while we have snow."

"If Osip is to tell his tale, he will tell it in his own way." The peasant youth looked down sternly at Peter, who quickly subsided.

"Now, as we all agree," continued Osip, "there is no land where the winter snow does not fall, so our friends the Ox, the Ram, the Pig, and the Goose were merely looking for pike [fish] in the tops of trees. Winter overtook them on the way. The Ox said, 'Friends, we have been deceived. We have traveled far; yet we find winter here too. Let us stop and build a house.' But the others were stubborn and would not stop. They laughed at the Ox when he stayed behind to build his house.

"First there was snow. Then the wind began to blow, bringing with it the bitter cold from the Frost King's country. The poor Pig grunted wretchedly, the Ram ran about in circles trying to keep his blood from curdling, and the Goose flapped her wings dismally. Finally they turned back, and when they came to the Ox's house, they all cried out together, 'Dear Friend Ox, please let us in. We are freezing.'

" 'Go away,' bellowed the Ox. You see, he was pretty much displeased with the way he had been laughed at.

" 'If you don't let us in, I shall butt my head against your door until it lies in splinters and the north wind freezes you!' threatened the Ram.

" 'Hum,' thought the Ox. 'The Ram's argument has a lawyer's logic.' But he called out, 'You shall not come in. I can certainly handle one Ram.'

" 'Then I shall dig the dirt away from the walls of your house until they fall in on you,' threatened the Pig.

" 'This fellow is a very statesman for good arguments,' thought the Ox. But he called out, 'You shall not come in. I can certainly handle one Pig.'

" 'Then I shall fly up and sit on your chimney, so that all the smoke will come back into the room and choke you,' threatened the Goose.

" 'That fellow is a very philosopher for clever reasoning,' thought the Ox. But he called out, 'You shall not come in. I can certainly handle one Goose.'

"The Pig and the Ram and the Goose consulted together. Then they called out with one voice, 'Beware, Friend Ox! We shall not do these things singly. We shall come all together, butting and burrowing and roosting on your chimney!'

" 'Ah, me,' thought the Ox. 'These fellows are not clever lawyers, statesmen, and philosophers. They are just ordinary folks using horse sense.' And he called out, 'You shall come in. You have convinced me with your arguments.'

"And so they all lived together during the winter. They were such good friends all this time that each felt quite safe in sleeping with only one eye open.

"And then! *Then* there came a bear, howling outside their house and clawing at the door.

" 'What shall we do?' The Ox looked at his companions in fright. 'Not one of us here is strong enough to kill Bruin.'
" 'Not one, but all together,' said the Goose wisely. 'When the bear breaks down the door, we shall rush at him all at once. You, Friend Ox, shall do the goring with those sharp horns of yours and pin Bruin to the wall. Ram will pound him breathless with his hard head. Pig will worry him with his bristly snout, and I—I shall peck at his eyes!'

"And so it happened, and old Bruin was so gored and pounded and worried and pecked that he was glad to escape at last with some of his skin whole.

"And the Ox and the Ram and the Pig and the Goose went on living happily enough in the little hut, waiting for the spring to come to the frozen land. But whether they waited a short time or a long time, there is no way of telling."

"Da, da." The old cook nodded and sighed as she gave Osip his cup of tea. "You will find yourself some day in the salt mines in Siberia, you with your tales."

The children puzzled over her speech but could make nothing of it. They did not understand that Osip, a serf, one of the poverty-ridden slaves of the Tsar, longed for freedom and dared to speak to other serfs about his ideas. Like the animals of his little fable, he saw that all the serfs would have to move together to strike off their chains; but, for such ideas, men in Tsarist Russia were flogged or sent to the prison camps of the frozen north.

The children were presently called upstairs to have tea with the family. While Osip was winding up his tale, the Frost King had ceased shaking his beard. Peter ran to the window of the living-room and looked out on fields of white stretching as far as eye could see. The sun showed its face, casting long evening shadows wherever pine tree or fence post

stood. Peter was still at the window when the sound of distant
singing became audible.

"They've come!" cried Peter Ilich, his eyes lighting up and
glowing as if a fire burned behind them. "Father, Mother,
Mademoiselle! They're coming! Do listen!"

"*Mon Dieu!*" Fanny Dürbach exclaimed, noticing the
alarming change in her young pupil. "What is it? What is
happening?"

Father Ilya heard her from the entrance way, where he was
kicking the snow from his boots, and called up the stairway.
"It's the miners come to sing the *kolyady* for us," he shouted.
"The singers usually come on Christmas Eve, but there has
been sickness in the huts—something contagious—so they
waited to ask my permission. My orders, you know. Can't
have my family exposed to sickness from the mines."

"But what are *kolyady?*" the governess wanted to know as
Father Ilya joined the family in the dining room.

"Very ancient songs, Mademoiselle—shepherds' songs and
carols. This should be a rare treat for you. The singers go all
around to well-to-do households. The custom is to give them
food. Then they will go away without doing you some mischief, such as taking your gate off its hinges."

Fanny Dürbach laughed. "It is like the English custom of
caroling and playing Hallowe'en pranks all in one."

Mother Alexandra spoke up suddenly. "Calm yourself,
Pierre. No need for such excitement over a little music."

By this time all the children had their noses pressed to the
windows, the better to see the procession. Men with their
wives and their children were moving on sleds and on foot
toward the big house. They were carrying torches made of
pine splinters. All the men were singing, some in the curious
Slavic high voices, some in the magnificent Russian basses
which are the lowest voices in the world.

Mother Alexandra gave Hippolite and Sasha into the care of the old grandmother and hurried down to busy herself in the kitchen, seeing to it that the gifts of sausage, nuts, chicken, and sweets (the traditional reward of the *kolyady* singers) were in readiness.

> "Woman, give me eggs and cakes;
> Else your fences we will break!"

The children laughed to hear the impudent threat of the merry Christmas song.

"Monsieur Tchaikovsky," whispered the governess, "do look at our little Peter Ilich."

Peter had left his post at the window. He was sitting apart from the family group, a thoughtful expression in his deep blue eyes. He was beating out time with one slender hand while he hummed to himself the melody which was growing very loud as the singers came into the yard.

Father Ilya frowned a little even as he smiled fondly at his son. "Do you know, Mademoiselle Fanny, I believe we should get a music teacher for Petrushka. He has learned every waltz his mother knows. And as for the orchestrion which I had sent from St. Petersburg—" he pointed to a large music box standing near the stove—"the boy can play every air it tinkles out, even Zerlina's song from Mozart's *Magic Flute*."

Peter forgot his humming and beating time when the lusty peasants came tramping up the stairway. They were a rough, ragged lot, wearing sheepskin coats and fur hats, and felt boots so large and padded that feet and legs looked more like tree trunks than anything human. Ice particles clung to the men's beards, and there were frozen tears on the women's faces. Cheeks and noses had been nipped apple-red, and lips were dry and cracked from the raw weather.

Seeing the Tchaikovsky children, the peasants began a song old as the time-worn Ural Mountains, older even than Mother Volga. "Grandfather Pahom" it was called. No Russian child but knows about Grandfather Pahom, a kind of demon Santa Claus, who takes presents away instead of bringing them. The song tells how he wears a cap that looks like a crow's nest and has a beard like a horse's tail. And on his feet he wears sandals that were made by the devil himself on a moonlight night.

The children laughed gleefully, for Grandfather Pahom is just a make-believe goblin, and no one takes him very seriously. Even when the deep voices of the bass singers muttered "Woe, woe, nothing but woe!" and the singers shook their fingers at the children as much as to say, "Look out! Or Grandfather Pahom will steal away all your nice gifts!" no one minded any more than English and American children mind the pumpkin faces and the ghost tales on Hallowe'en.

After the Grandfather Pahom song, the singers returned to the kitchen for the gifts which, like the strange fairy creature of whom they had been singing, they carried away with them.

During the singing Peter's attention had been caught by a boy his own age. The child had cried softly to himself because his hands were too cold. The music instantly lost its charm for Peter. The sight of suffering was always unbearable for him, and all the sunshine of the day would disappear at the sight of a beggar or a starved kitten. Everywhere in old Russia suffering was a common sight; for this was the land where poor people were slaves—"serfs." On the farms they were forced to work all their lives for rich landlords who paid them meagerly in food and shelter and richly in lashings with the cruel Russian whip called a knout. They could not run away from ill-treatment, for serfs were "bound to the soil."

They were considered to be as permanent a part of a farm as the barns or plows. The singers on this very Christmas Eve were serfs, peasant-slaves of the Tsar, forced to labor long hours in the copper mines of Votkinsk.

When the last of the *kolyady* singers had gone, Mother Alexandra returned to take charge of Sasha and Hippolite. Peter shyly crept into the large chair beside his grandmother. His face was serious, for he was still troubled by thoughts of the crying child.

"Well, my little dove. I suppose it is a tale you want." Grandmother ran her wrinkled fingers through her favorite grandson's wayward hair.

Peter nodded gratefully, and the other children crowded eagerly around the kindly old lady.

"Nu, then! Listen well and I shall tell you about the Frost King's Bride. The chill winds from Tatary sing their strange Chinese songs to the pines beside the well, and that is how mortal folk get to know about such fairy people as Morosko the Frost King. The song that the winds sing in memory of the Frost King's Bride is an old, old song:

"Oh, the Frost King's nose is red as rust
And ice hangs from his hair;
But the Frost King's Bride comes in silver and gold,
And the Frost King's Bride is fair!

Oh, the Frost King's Bride comes in silver and gold,
And the Frost King's Bride will not be cold,
Though her head and feet be bare!"

Thus the old grandmother began the folk tale which, though it may differ in small details when it is told in Siberia or in Astrakhan, in Tiflis or in Moscow, is always recognizable in its essential details. It is really the story, in dramatic and allegorical form, of winter and the ever-present danger of freezing if one is far from home. In this old *skazka*, a young girl is tricked into going into the forest, and there she is left to freeze. She is at first very cold, and she weeps forlornly; but presently the Frost King takes pity on her and makes her warm and sleepy. Though she is stiff and cold by morning, those who find her are consoled; for they know that she is really the Frost King's Bride.

> And the Frost King's Bride will not be cold,
> Though her head and feet be bare!

"So ends the story of Morosko and his bride," said old *matushka*. "You have heard it as my mother told it to me, my mother who heard it from her mother's mother, who had it from an old grandmother, who learned the tale from a Cossack, who had got it from a Gypsy, whose great-great-great-great-great-grandfather was Morosko the Frost King himself. So you see, it must be true, and if you don't believe it, then you don't believe that Ivan the Fool and Humpy his little horse found the feather of the Firebird!"

"Tell us, tell us!" cried the children. "Tell us about Ivan."

But the old grandmother only laughed and pretended to go to sleep.

So that prin - ces and no - bles and lords may heark - en well,

3

One of the rooms at Votkinsk had been converted into a schoolroom for the children. Tables and chairs, maps and charts, cases of books, and shelves for copybooks, pens, and ink bottles—these gave the square old room with its heavy draperies at the windows and its huge corner stove a scholarly air of orderliness and purpose.

On an early spring day in the year 1846, Peter and Nicholas and Lidia spread their books and papers on the tables with none of their usual zest. They kept looking longingly at the windows, through which they could see clouds piling up like lamb's fleece in a sky as blue as flax flowers. The pen in Peter's hand made round un-Russian letters in his copybook; for his mind was on the swallows returning from the south.

Their tutor, the good Blinof, seemed to be disturbed by thoughts of the spring, too. He stood with his back to his young pupils, looking out absently into the branches of a tall pine. A brisk spring wind frolicked in the branches, causing them to weave about crazily.

Lidia's and Nicholas' whispering attracted his wandering attention. He said, without turning, "Attend to your compositions, please. Take more care with your letters, Peter Ilich." Peter's face was a comical study in amazement. How, he wondered, could Blinof know that his letters were not right without even turning to look? Dutifully he set to work again to copy the little four-line poem by the great Russian poet Pushkin. *Vecher* (The Wind), it was called.

> Wind, O Wind, you giant!
> How you blow the clouds about.
> How you lash the blue seas,
> You who sweep everywhere in the vast open places.

As he wrote he was thinking: How I should like to be outdoors right now with Wind the Giant. He is blowing those great clouds past the window. He is free to run through the world, and we have to sit in this stuffy room and learn how to write Russian. Without knowing it, Peter frowned as he thought these rebellious thoughts. Catching sight of his young pupil's thoroughly unhappy face, Blinof relented.

"Enough writing for today," he announced and smiled to see the speed with which books and copybooks were closed and pen and ink laid away on the shelves. "How would you like for me to read you some of the great Russian poems? We have about half an hour before Mademoiselle Dürbach comes to take you for a walk."

The children smiled their acceptance of the idea, and Blinof drew a slender volume from his coat pocket. The tutor had read and studied this book a great deal, it seemed, for the pages were marked with notes and the corners dog-eared.

"First of all," said Blinof, "a poem by Alexander Pushkin. Young Peterkin has been copying some of his verses today."

The tutor smiled down at Peter's earnest face. How the child was growing, Blinof thought to himself. Just six years old; yet as he stood beside the tutor's chair their eyes were on a level.

"Which of you can tell me something about Pushkin?"

Lidia spoke up promptly. "He came from a wealthy family, but he chose to spend most of his time listening to the stories and the songs of the peasants. He wrote a poem once that got him into trouble—the Tsar exiled him to the Caucasus Mountains for it—but later he was allowed to come back to St. Petersburg. He wrote plays and short stories and novels and poems, and he was very witty and handsome, and he was killed in a duel."

Blinof laughed delightedly. "Well, well, Lidia. That is a biography all in one bean-pod. Well remembered! But what about Pushkin's writings. Can you name me some of the longer works, Nicholas?"

Nicholas could name three: *Boris Godunov*, *The Queen of Spades*, and *Eugene Oniegin*.

"Good enough, Kolya. Now for our reading. Let me see. Ah, here is a good one. It may be a little over your heads, but sometimes it is good for us to stand on tiptoe and try to reach the meanings of things."

Blinof read with expression and deep appreciation, and the children, taking his advice, stood on mental tiptoe to glimpse the meaning now and again of the grown-up thought.

THE CUP OF LIFE

More bitter than the lees of new-pressed wine
　　The vain remembrance of long-dead delight.
　　But even as wine ripens with time's flight
So glows my spirit with the day's decline.
Though looms the morrow fearsome and malign,
　　A sunless waste of dread adversity.

Yet not for restful death I craven cry,
But fain would live and drink Life's cup divine.

This is my prayer: To suffer, to create,
    And know the ecstasy of blind desires.
Through lowering clouds of unrelenting fate
    To hear the voices of ethereal lyres;
Till from Love's golden cup is drunk the wine,
Then welcome Death—Life's wondrous draught was mine!

Blinof looked up from the book thoughtfully. "That such
a man," he remarked, "should have died in a senseless duel!"
He turned over some pages, "Ah, here is one that will please
you. It is a verse-fable by our great satirist Krylov, who died
just two years ago. It is called 'Chaos.' "

> "A Swan, a Pike, and Crab one day
>   Combined together all
> And harnessed to a cart, they say,
>   Essayed a load to haul.
>
> But though they tugged with main and might
> The cart within the mire stuck tight.
>
> Up to the sky the Swan did fly,
>   The Crab did sideways crawl,
> Straight for the Sea the Pike did hie
>   Which proved of value small.
>
> Now who was most to blame, I swear
>   I really cannot say;
> The moral plain—the cart is there,
>   Embedded to this day!"

A merry laugh from the doorway brought Blinof to his feet.
Fanny Dürbach had slipped in quietly during the reading of

the fable, and now she exclaimed, "Krylov's little creatures should have borrowed a page from Osip's story of the Ox, the Ram, the Pig, and the Goose, I think."

The children went scampering down the hall to find their coats; for the spring wind was freshening as the day drew toward its close. Mademoiselle Dürbach in her chic bonnet and trim black coat from Paris stayed for a moment's conversation with Blinof.

"Seriously," she said, "ought you to be so open with your admiration for such ideas? This Russia—*ma foi!* it is an unhappy place. So much suffering and injustice! And yet I think I should not have the courage to speak out as Osip does, for instance."

"Those who are afraid of wolves should not go into the forest," growled the tutor, and they dropped the subject.

Nicholas and Lidia and Peter Ilich, done up in thick coats, caps, mufflers, mittens, and boots, looked like bear cubs come out of their winter cave to sniff the sharp spring air. Fanny Dürbach hustled them along in her gay, brisk way, directing the walk past the ugly dumps and dismal buildings of the copper mines toward the hills where patches of snow still lay in the hollows and under the spruces and pines.

On the way, they passed a row of small houses of wood weathered to a dirty gray. Several children playing in front of one of the houses stopped to watch the group from the big house. Fanny Dürbach and her little brood felt uncomfortable as they suffered this sharp scrutiny; for even as they laughed and talked about the little happenings of the day they were all the while aware of the difference between their lot and that of the ragged waifs who lived in the workers' huts attached to the mines.

The peasant children had no boots, Peter noticed; their feet were wrapped with layer upon layer of felt strips so that the result suggested something misshapen and deformed. A little girl, whose uncombed hair was partially covered by a soiled red-and-blue kerchief, very badly needed another kerchief to wipe her nose.

Contrasts of extreme poverty with comfort have a way of making the sunshine of a spring day less bright. The governess and her children were a little less gay as they walked on toward the barracks where the Cossack troops were quartered.

The children had been used all their lives to the sight of these husky "policemen of the Tsar" with the smart belted coats, tall fur caps, and gleaming sabers; so Peter and Nicholas and Lidia gave no thought to why a hundred of these hard-riding, fearless, reckless troops should be stationed all the time at Votkinsk. Fanny Dürbach, however, was thinking of the serfs working the mines; and she knew full well that the Tsar's most merciless soldiers were there to see that the miners worked well and long, that none among them started to grumble, that anyone like Osip who suggested that conditions might be improved should be shot or whipped or perhaps sent into the more terrible mines of Siberia. The French governess knew these things, but she also recalled Blinof's proverb: "Those who are afraid of wolves should not go into the forest."

Strange, strange country, she was thinking: Overworked serfs, kept in line by Cossacks from the Don and Dnieper and Bug River valleys—and over all this the Inspector of Mines, father of her pupils, a kindly man who on his own account and of his own wish would not have hurt a fly. How could such things be?

As they passed the Cossack barracks, two or three young huskies came out to mount sleek black horses tethered to the fence. Catching sight of the pretty young governess, they saluted with mock seriousness and laughed hearty, booming laughs at her confusion. They struck up a song as they trotted away. The color and movement and lusty liveliness of the scene and the amazing beauty of the voices held Peter spellbound.

The Cossack song told about a slain soldier for whom "Lo, a fair sister weeps and a mother mourns":

THE SLAIN COSSACK

O, ye wide rolling plains
O, ye fair green fields,
Where the tall grass waves,
And the wild heather blows!

All is purple and green,
All is peace and rest,
Save for one, bleak lonely grove,
Where the wild willows bend.

Fanny Dürbach shook her head, puzzled. Professional soldiers and slave-drivers, how could they sing with such beauty? Surely, surely, she thought, all men have poetry in them, and some day—when life itself may be easier and kinder to all—even such as these will no longer find it necessary to deny this poetry by violent acts.

Cheered by this thought, the governess stepped out even more briskly so that the children had to hop and skip to keep pace with her.

"Will there be any snowdrops, do you think, Mademoiselle?" Peter found breath between hops to ask wistfully after his favorite of the early flowers.

"Hardly, Pierre. Next month, perhaps. See, even the birch trees are without leaves, and the wild geese are just beginning to return to their marshes."

Before they reached the woods, the wind veered and changed into one of the raw southeasters which blow out of Asia. Noticing that Peter, who in growing so tall had also grown too thin for the Russian cold, was shivering and looking blue under his eyes, the governess turned back.

"Nearly time for dinner," she announced. "And remember? Some of our neighbors are coming over, and Madame your mother told me just before we came for our walk that if you are all very good you may eat with the grown-ups today and stay for the music afterward."

Peter capered in the road with delight. The mud that had splashed the children's boots on the way from the house was freezing, and ice crunched underfoot as they walked over the little water-filled hollows of the ruts.

The lamps were already lit when Fanny and the children reached the house. A buzz of conversation and soft laughter issued from the music-room as they passed the door on the way to change their clothes.

Lidia put on the dainty French frock she had received at Christmas, and the boys put on fresh blouses. Even Sasha, who was now four years old, was allowed to come out of the nursery and join the older children.

Peter was first to be ready, probably because he had given

only a lick and a promise to his ears and neck and put his blouse on hind-side-to.

"For shame, Pierre," said his mother, coming swiftly toward the doorway to make her son a little more presentable before she introduced him to the guests. "Why can't you be neat and tidy like Nicholas? Well, I suppose we must let the blouse pass. There—perhaps you will do," she added, brushing his unruly hair out of his eyes.

"This is Peter Ilich, my son who is musical," she told the group assembled in the music-room.

Peter bowed the stiff little bow which he had been taught was a part of correct manners, and looked shyly about. The room was quite crowded. A number of smart young Russian officers, technical men in the service of the government just as Peter's father was, laughed together in groups. Maria Palchikova, the timid young music teacher whom Father Ilya had hired for Peter, was making herself as inconspicuous as possible. The cultivated English family who lived in a large house beyond the mines were there, speaking Russian with the accent that always made Peter and the rest of the children smile secretly.

"Time for just one more tune," Father Ilya said heartily. "Then we shall have dinner."

Mother and her guests had formed themselves into an impromptu orchestra. Mother and Maria took turns at the piano. Father insisted on bringing out his flute, though he could not play one tune clear through and was usually out of time and rhythm. The young officers had brought various kinds of musical instruments—violins, cellos, and several *balalaikas*, those curious triangular guitars of Russia.

Mother's repertoire consisted solely of simple waltzes, and Maria's skill was hardly greater. The other instruments followed the lead of the piano, and the result was hardly the finest music. What the musicians lacked in technique, however, they made up in hearty good humor. Peter drank in every note, and pretended to be directing the orchestra in the way Blinof had told him the conductors of the orchestras in St. Petersburg and Moscow did.

The music whirled in Peter's head all during dinner. Afterward, when Maria and Mother played and the rest danced, he became more and more excited. Mademoiselle Dürbach noticed that his cheeks were too flushed and his eyes too bright.

"Come, Pierre. Time for bed, I think."

Peter did not demur. The excitement of the evening was becoming painful to his sensitive nerves. He was a long while getting to sleep. Fanny came upstairs once to look in at him and found him sitting up in bed crying to himself.

"Pierre! What is wrong?"

"Oh, Mademoiselle, this music! This music! Save me from it! It is here"—he pointed to his head—"and will not give me any peace."

Fanny Dürbach soothed her little pupil into a flushed sleep. As she returned to the company downstairs she thought back to that Christmas when the *kolyady* singers had excited Peter Ilich so strangely. She remembered how eagerly he had learned the waltzes his mother taught him, how every spare moment was spent at the piano, where he made up little tunes. She recalled how he would stay at the piano for hours unless he were forced to go for a walk or to play with the other children. He had been stubborn on one of these occasions, refusing to go out to play when his mother closed the piano. Instead, he had stood moodily at the window, beating out the time of some melody in his head on the window pane. So hard and fast did his rhythmic fingers drum on the window that the glass broke, and Peter was cut painfully. It was after this incident that the music teacher Maria was engaged.

"Surely," decided Fanny Dürbach, "we have a great talent among us. What a pity it should be a talent for music!"

Lo! the tall and val-iant cham-pions came from far and near;

4

The extravagant Russian summer was coming to its close. The luxuriant wild grasses that covered the plains were scattering their brittle seed to the wind. Wild cherries and wild apricots had already spread a banquet for the birds, and the willow catkins were making their airy voyages to find likely earthen harbors when the snow came to cover them. The deer were seen less frequently in the foothills than they would be later, when the heavy snows in the mountains would drive them to lower country. Little animals—squirrels and hares and marmots—were having a harvest festival in the fields and groves. The wild duck rose like clouds from the marshes of the Kama River, and the wild geese flew high against the sun on their way south for the winter.

Nicholas, Peter, and Lidia had been walking with Fanny Dürbach along the banks of the Kama.

"See," said the governess in playful mood. "The water of our river hurries a little here. It has a long journey before it, and doubtless wishes to make it before the frost comes."

"Where does the river go, Mademoiselle?" Peter wanted to know.

"South and east of here, Pierre, until it joins the Volga River—Mother Volga as your folk-songs call it. Then both rivers together are called the Volga, and this large stream flows south through Samara, and Saratof, and on south to Astrakhan on the Caspian Sea."

Lidia broke into the geography lesson. "Isn't it nearly time for tea, Mademoiselle? I feel so hollow—and yet I don't see how I shall be able to swallow a bite, I'm so excited and jumpy inside my skin. Just think, this is the day Zinaïda is coming home!"

Zinaïda was the half-sister of Nicholas, Peter, Sasha, and Hippolite, the daughter of their father's first marriage. She had been at school in St. Petersburg, at the Catherine's Institute, but now her schooling was at an end and she was coming home to stay.

"Yes, it is nearly time for tea. But Zinaïda may not be here for many hours yet—indeed, she may not get here today." Mademoiselle Dürbach was remembering all too vividly the delays of her three-weeks' trip from St. Petersburg with Mother Tchaikovsky and Nicholas. "But anyway, come along. We must not keep the samovar waiting. After tea, we shall have time for a short history lesson. Stories this time, not just dry dates and treaties," she added laughing, seeing Nicholas' face grow long.

Nicholas was immediately cheered, for Mademoiselle Dürbach was clever at weaving the events of history into dramatic stories, and making the women and men and children of long ago seem human and real and warmly alive.

Tea and cheese and bread were brought to the children in the summerhouse in the garden. Four-year-old Sasha came running from the house to join the older children, and Hippolite's angry wails from within plainly showed that young two-year-old's displeasure at being restrained from following.

The vines which had made a green umbrella for the little summerhouse in midsummer were dry and rattling against the boards, and the sun fell in large warm patches on the table and food and on Mademoiselle Dürbach's smooth hair. The children ate hungrily and were soon done.

When the tea things were cleared away, the governess opened a bag that lay on the bench beside her. Out of it she took a piece of linen on which she was working a design in red and black and yellow thread. It was an odd pattern of sunflowers, which grow like weeds in the fields of Russia, and of stiff, unnatural animals that were probably supposed to be deer. Fanny Dürbach had discovered this design on a scarf of the cook's—a hand-woven scarf that had belonged to the cook's mother. Fanny had copied off this bit of peasant art to remind her in years to come of the days she had spent in Votkinsk.

"Will you run and bring the big atlas for us, Pierre?" she asked. "I am going to tell you some tales about your own great land of Russia, and as I talk I want you children to look at the maps."

Peter was away like a rabbit, and returned to the garden breathless, carrying an unwieldy atlas under his arm. Quickly, to show that he knew how to do things, he opened the huge book and sat holding it on his lap as Fanny Dürbach began her stories.

First of all she talked about the ancient peoples who inhabited the land. "They were Slavs," she said, "a people interested chiefly in the arts of peace. They disliked warring, wanted nothing so much as to be left alone in their wooden villages to till their fields and on feast days to bring out the old harps and sing melancholy songs from the half-remembered past. They had established large settlements at the sites of present Novgorod, Rostov, Kiev, and Smolensk.

"The Slavs had, in their desire to be left alone, closed the doors to their neighbors. But there were three windows in their house which they failed to take into account. These windows were three rivers and their valleys: The Neva, which connects Lake Ladoga with the Baltic Sea in the north; the Dnieper, which flows through Kiev to the Black Sea; and the Volga, which receives tributaries from beyond the Ural Mountains and flows into the Caspian Sea.

"Warlike neighbors came through these windows to harry the peace-loving Slavs. Many a fair youth singing as he worked in some green field had his song stilled forever by a savage blow from a wandering tribesman riding up from the south or east.

"From the north—through the first window—across the Baltic to the Neva and so into Lake Ladoga, came the fierce, blue-eyed Vikings, or Varangians as they were called in the old Russian chronicles. They were roving bands, who had goods to trade. Some of these Vikings settled in the larger towns, and soon these reckless exiles from Scandinavia made themselves at home. It was no trick for the aggressive North-men to dominate the Slavs; and indeed the Slavs were rather glad to ask three of the Varangian princes to rule over them—Rurik, Sineus, and Truvor. This, the old chronicles tell us, was in the ninth century.

"In his dragon ship Rurik came, he with the arm strong enough to fell an ox, he of the beard red as the dusty sky at sunset and eyes bluer than the icebergs drifting down from the Pole. He and his brothers came to trade in the land of the Slavs and remained to be kings. It was not long before Rurik was king alone, for he was one to have his way in all things.

"In the next century, Queen Olga, who ruled the Slavs

from her palace at Kiev, sailed in a royal boat down the Dnieper, and with all her retinue proceeded to Constantinople. There she became converted to Christianity, and was baptized in the Greek Catholic Church. Back up the Dnieper she sailed, and thus through this second window came a new religion to take the place of the worship of Perun the Thunder God, and the other nature gods of the Slavs.

"In the thirteenth century, the third window opened, and the Tatars poured onto the Russian steppes from Asia. They appeared first in the southeast, moving as one man. These were the 'Golden Hordes' of Genghis Khan and the Khans that came after him. Following the great Khan's death, his people continued to press westward and northward into Russia until they threatened Moscow, or Muscovy, stronghold of powerful princes.

"Plunging into the deep forests of the Volga, the Tatar chieftains met the envoys from Muscovy. They were brave and determined, the Moscow princes, and fearlessly they strode toward the silk-lined tents and oriental carts of the encamped invaders.

" 'We come in peace,' announced the Muscovites.

" 'If you want peace, give us the tenth of your goods each year,' returned the Tatar chiefs.

" 'When we are dead, then you can have the whole,' replied the angered princes and returned to their own camps.

"And so the Tatar armies loosed their fury on the armies of Moscow. The Russian princes had never seen men fight as the Tatars did. The Mongols were arranged in five ranks, widely separated. The first two ranks were in full armor, mounted, and their horses were in armor, too. The armored men carried lances. The last three ranks did not wear armor, and they fought with bow and javelin.

"In battle, the first two ranks rushed upon the battle line

of the enemy. The rear ranks poured through the intervals in the front ranks and raised a hail of arrows and javelins on the opposing forces. This first rush, followed by the heavy barrage of arrows and javelins, would inevitably disorganize the enemy. Immediately the enemy's lines wavered, and the front ranks of the Tatar army rushed in to deliver the crushing blow.

"Thus many of the Muscovite princes and thousands of their followers were killed, and those who were left were glad enough to pay tribute. Even fearless Alexander Nevsky, who earned his last name because he repulsed the invading German hordes on the frozen Neva River, was forced eventually to bow his proud head and pay tribute to the Khans.

"For two and a half centuries the Tatars ruled Russia, interfering little with the customs and religion and personal freedom of the people as long as the levy of the tenth part of Russian goods was paid. Gradually, Moscow rose again to power. The son of Alexander Nevsky, Daniel Dolgoruki, proved more than a match for Tatar cunning, and what he began, Ivan the Great finished—the task of making Moscow once and for all the real capital of Russia, free of the Tatar yoke.

"And so," concluded Fanny Dürbach, laying aside her sewing, "that is how three great peoples—the Slavs, the Northmen, and the Tatars—all helped to form this great land. It is a wonderful cultural heritage you have, my dears, rich in folk-lore, folk-music, poetry, and drama. Some day you will understand exactly what I mean."

Peter with the atlas on his lap had been absorbed in the tales of long ago. Suddenly he began to spit on the map of Europe.

"Pierre!" cried Mademoiselle Dürbach in horror. "What has come over you, spitting on a beautiful book?"

"I spit on all countries that are not Russia!" Peter said, fiercely earnest.

"But, Peter, that is not why I told you the historical tales! Other countries have history, too. And there are boys and girls very like you in the German states, in Italy and France, in Switzerland, and in Turkey and far-away China, too. Besides, if you hate everyone outside of Russia, you must hate people in France. And that means you hate me, for I am French, and your mother, too, who is French—Assière was her name, you know, and your grandfather settled in Russia not so many years ago!"

"Mademoiselle, there is no need to scold me. Didn't you see me cover France with my hand first?"

The governess laughed in spite of herself, but she shook her head seriously all the same. Peter's eyes fell before hers, and he no longer took pride in what he had done.

Fanny Dürbach once said of this favorite pupil of hers: "His sensibility was extreme. A trifle wounded him deeply. He was as brittle as porcelain."

Her lesson was not lost on such a boy. In later years, though he always loved his own country best, he traveled extensively, even as far as America, and among his good friends he numbered Norwegians and French and Swiss, English, Germans, and Americans, and people of many other nationalities as well.

The little group in the summerhouse were sent flying to the front gate when they heard the creak of carriage wheels and the sound of horses trotting along the dusty road. The coach drew up before the Tchaikovsky house, and Zinaïda jumped down to greet her family. Simply but smartly dressed in her schoolgirl's uniform, carrying an armload of bundles that held presents for the family, full of strange mannerisms and fashionable expressions, she was to the minds of Nicholas and Lidia and Peter the very breath of St. Petersburg, that mysterious city to the west, city of romance and adventure.

Zinaïda was the center of attention as the family gathered round the dining-room table, where the inevitable samovar and tall glasses had been set out. Mother asked eagerly after friends and relatives in St. Petersburg, the city which was her home, the place to which her French father had emigrated with his family after the French Revolution. Her youth had been spent in a school for orphans, for after her parents' death she had been quite alone except for a younger brother and sister. These two, Mikhail and Yekaterina Assier, lived in St. Petersburg. They had sent many messages and presents with Zinaïda.

When Zinaïda had delivered all the messages and answered all the questions, she talked about school and her young friends. The Tchaikovsky children listened open-mouthed to descriptions of the theater, the opera, and the ballet, which Zinaïda and her schoolgirl companions had attended under the watchful eyes of chaperones and tutors from the school.

"What is a ballet?" Peter wanted to know.

Zinaïda tried to describe how young men and women, trained from childhood in the curious art of dancing on the tips of their toes, acted out in pantomime quaint fairy tales and romantic episodes from dramatic works. She laughed as she realized how impossible it was to give an idea in words of the light fanciful music which sent these dancers whirling through their stories. "What grace and beauty! And the music and color!" she finished rather lamely.

Her meager description had been enough, nevertheless, to set Peter's imagination on fire. He envisioned the dancers in their flower-soft costumes and dainty satin slippers sweeping like wind-blown leaves across the huge stage. He saw them moving sometimes quietly and with infinite grace, sometimes bending and leaping with athletic ease, sometimes whirling madly in a dance of exotic rhythms.

Peter edged himself away from the family group and sat down at the piano. His fingers touched the keys lightly, making them sing out frisky little melodies, full of youthful chuckling. For him the somber room with the heavy table and the copper samovar had been transformed into a brilliant stage, where fairy-tale creatures—Puss in Boots, Sleeping Beauty, the Frog-Prince, the Frost King's Bride, Ivan and Humpy who found the feather of the Firebird, the Moon Princess, all the Puckish and dainty fairy folk from the land of Oberon— told their stories in graceful or rakish pantomime, and flower- like dancers moved with artful grace as the tale unfolded.

"*Nu!*" Zinaïda uttered the familiar Russian exclamation. Setting down her glass of tea, she turned to look at her half- brother in surprise. "Is he making that up as he goes?" she asked.

"For *hours* he will sit there, if you let him," Mother Alex- andra explained almost apologetically. "He does have talent," she added wistfully.

"He looks pale," decided practical Zinaïda. "You probably let him sit there too much. Everyone makes a pet of him, no doubt."

Of all the family, Zinaïda was the only one who did not let Peter have his way. Indeed, in the years to come Peter often had reason to remember her reproaches and sharp unfavor- able comments on his ways.

"Peter Ilich! You have played enough! Stop now."

Peter obeyed, though he was irritated by the brusqueness of the command. He slipped out of the room, opened the heavy front door, and sat down gloomily on the porch. It was dark outside by this time. A light breeze rustled the leaves of the vines and trees of the garden. Peter listened attentively to all the sounds of the night—the hooting of an owl somewhere, the twittering of a bird finding its evening shelter, the rasping call of crickets in the grass. He had forgotten his little trouble and was humming quietly to himself when Fanny Dürbach shook him gently by the shoulder.

Evening was always to have a special place in Peter Ilich's moods. Years later he expressed his love of the quiet of night in songs like these:

SLEEPLESS NIGHTS

WINTER EVENING

For my fate calls me forth on a jour-ney far and wide,

5

$\mathcal{I}$n early October of the year 1848, the uneventful, ordered life at Votkinsk came to an abrupt end. Father Ilya Tchaikovsky decided to resign his position as Government Inspector of Mines and go to Moscow, where he expected to apply for a position with a private mining firm. Negotiations had been going forward by letter, and there seemed no doubt that he would receive the appointment.

Lidia's father established a household again, and arrangements were made for Grandmother and Lidia to stay in the Urals region with him. Peter and the rest of the children were excited at the prospect of seeing a large city. They helped cheerfully with the packing, though they tried the patience of their busy mother sorely by being too much underfoot.

Mother Alexandra had her hands full, what with her large family and the hundred and one tasks connected with closing a big house. Good-natured Father Ilya could not help inviting friends home for dinner—young engineers, the English family, the neighboring mine officials and owners, anyone he happened to meet as he drove about in his carriage on business for the mines. Patient Mother Alexandra sometimes bit her lip in vexation, and spoke her mind in private; but she never failed in her courtesy to guests. In the midst of crating furniture, and packing glassware in barrels and clothing in trunks, she somehow found time to plan dinners and suppers for the veritable "court" that Father Ilya held every evening.

At one of the evening gatherings, a young Polish officer was introduced to the family group. He was an excellent pianist, enthusiastic over the music of his famous compatriot Chopin.

Chopin's exquisite waltzes and stately mazurkas danced with infinite grace from under the fingers of the distinguished young Pole at Votkinsk. Eight-year-old Peter's cheeks flushed as he listened. Shyly he asked if the musician would leave the music sheets with him for a day or so.

Hour after hour Peter practiced the mazurkas which his Polish friend consented to leave with him. Several days later when the owner of the music returned, Peter played two of the compositions for him.

The Polish officer looked up sharply at the first note, and listened with growing pleasure to the boy's charming interpretation of the Chopin music. At the last note he kissed Peter affectionately.

"I never saw Peter so radiantly happy as on that day," Fanny Dürbach once said.

It was not so easy to leave Votkinsk after all. The evening before the departure Peter looked out of his window toward the Cossack barracks. The soldiers had built campfires, round which they sat singing songs in lonesome minor keys.

Opening his window so that he might hear the singing clearly, Peter sat hugging his knees and shivering in the night air. Bright stars twinkled in the black sky. A few dim lights glowed from the peasant huts near the mine. The Cossacks' fires threw a ruddy glow over the men's faces and sent shadows dancing a Baba Yaga's (witch's) dance on the walls of the barracks. Mournfully their song "Alone in the Road" drifted toward the big house:

>"All alone, I wander through the foggy night;
>And my heart is lonely, in the night—
>Through the darkness must I go alone,
>Through the lonesome night, the lonesome night."

"The Setting Sun" was full of longing:

>"When on the water are seen the weeds,
>When on the water are swaying reeds—
>He sits alone, all alone is he,
>A lonesome Cossack, lone is he."

Fanny Dürbach was listening too, somewhat regretful that she was leaving the valley of the Kama River. The sad songs contributed to a growing unhappiness in her. She drew away from her window, impatient that these songs had power to affect her so. And yet why should they not? These were old songs, handed down to the reckless young soldiers at the camp by their parents and grandparents, the wild, free people who at an early time had rebelled against restraint and so had left more populous areas to live as free as the birds or wild animals along the Don and Dnieper rivers. Fierce longing for freedom, even at the price of bitter loneliness, was in these songs. And the will to be free is ever attractive.

Uneasiness lay in many a heart on the morning the family turned their backs once and for all on the home at Votkinsk. Saying good-by to Lidia and the old *matushka* was hard. When the house servants lined up to sing a sad song of farewell for them, all eyes glistened with tears.

A very real worry was tugging at Mother Alexandra's mind. Her husband, who trusted people implicitly, had told everyone far and near of the excellent job he expected to get when he made application in Moscow. Had this been a wise course? she wondered. There were others who looked forward to better jobs, too. Shrugging her shoulders, she tried to cast aside this worry. No need to build a bridge until you came to the water.

By carriage and by river boat the Tchaikovsky family proceeded from Votkinsk down the Kama River to its junction with the mighty Volga. The children were all eyes for the colorful life of the river. They saw lumber rafts by the hundreds manned by hard-muscled peasants who used long poles to keep the masses of logs from ramming into the banks of the river or settling on some sand bar.

On the river boat that took them to the Volga the passengers were mainly peasants from the farms of the district—*muzhiks* in red shirts, their wives and sisters and daughters in shapeless gathered skirts and cotton kerchiefs tied under their chins. These peasant folk kept up a ceaseless chewing of sunflower seeds. Handfuls of the striped seeds were thrown into cavernous mouths, and a steady stream of hulls were blown out, without, it seemed, any slowing up of the chewing process. Peter Ilich watched the chewers fascinated. Fanny Dürbach and his mother turned up their noses and lifted their skirts when they had to walk over the moistened hulls lying everywhere underfoot.

At the junction of the Kama and Volga, fish nets were spread out by the hundreds to dry under the sun. Men and women with the skill of lifelong practice worked with bobbins and heavy linen thread to close the ragged rents in the nets. The Volga fishermen wore quaint costumes that consisted of sleeveless leather jackets, with blouses extending below, and hip-high boots. They were mostly big bearded men with big voices. They called out heartily to the boat passengers and often sang snatches of folk-song. The wide stream was full of fishing boats, engaged in the greatest industry of the Volga basin—the catching of the giant sturgeon and the smaller sterlet, which furnish the famous Russian caviar.

Freight boats of all sizes and shapes, with every manner of merchandise from the Near East, plied their way upstream. Some had come from the far-away ports of the Caspian, and these, in addition to cargoes of the fine silky lamb's wool called by the name of the great city at the mouth of the Volga, Astrakhan, had passengers of many nationalities and foreign speech. Tatar merchants in rich silk-lined *kaftans* (robes). Turbaned Persians, with glistening black hair and villainous-looking mustaches. Bokharians in red robes and gorgeous turbans. Circassians in black robes, glittering with cartridge belts and silver-mounted daggers.

A motley, noisy crowd filled the boat which carried the Tchaikovsky family up-river toward Nizhni-Novgorod. Wherever the boat docked, passengers made a great to-do about buying bread, cheese, cucumbers, and lemons. The cheese was offered for sale in juglike cheese vases, the mouths covered with a sacklike cloth. Each passenger carried his own tea and sugar in a little bag, and usually a little teapot into which he drew hot water from the huge urns provided on board the boat. Bread and cheese, cucumbers and salted fish, washed down with hot tea was the standard meal. Personally, Peter Ilich thought he had never eaten anything quite so good.

A memorable experience for young Peter was the sight of a great raft loaded with grain being towed against the current by a long line of ragged men. These men walked the towpath with bare feet and tugged with straining muscles at the long tow lines. As they inched their way along, they sang songs of such poignant suffering and despair that Peter, fascinated though he was by their melancholy beauty, wished that he might run away from the sound. Of all the serfs in Russia, the *borlaki*, as the Volga boatmen were called, were the most miserable. Their misery found relief in such songs as "Down on Mother Volga," which Peter listened to almost against his will.

With each final "Ah!" the men threw themselves forward on the ropes with all their force, and the muscles on their legs and backs stood out like ugly knotted cords.

One of the songs the *borlaki* sang hammered its insistent melody deep into young Peter's mind. This was the song destined to become famous throughout the world, exciting the pity of every hearer, its sad melody telling the story of oppression in Russia more dramatically than words could have done. Like the Negro spirituals of America, which have universal appeal to all who have known sorrow and want, the "Volga Boat Song" has become the property of all peoples.

At Nizhni-Novgorod (modern Gorki, named for the famous Russian author Maxim Gorki) Mademoiselle took the older children sight-seeing. She pointed out the narrow spit of land between the junction of the Oka River with Mother Volga; on this point the famous fair of Nizhni was held in summer.

Thousands of people came to live on the point every year between June and September. The merchants set up hundreds of temporary shops and bazaars along the streets surrounding the building called the Glavny Dom, where the governor of the province stayed during the fair. In fair time, every nook and cranny of the town was filled with merchandise—skins and furs from Siberia, knives and daggers from the Caucasus, tea from China, Armenian, Persian, and Turkish rugs, and every manner of goods from the smart shops of Paris, London, Berlin, Vienna, Warsaw, and other centers of northern Europe.

The children looked wonderingly at the huge *kremlin* (fortress) with its walls sixty to ninety feet high, walls which had defied for many years the Golden Hordes from Tatary. Best of all they enjoyed their walk along the busy wharves, where hundreds of masts of tiny trading and fishing craft made Mother Volga's docks look like a forest of little trees. More than two hundred and fifty miles were yet to be covered when the family resumed its journey on the river boat from Nizhni. Part of the way was made in jolting post carriages, and the children grew tired and cross in the cramped seats which had taken the place of the wide boat decks. At one hamlet where the family stayed overnight, the inn where they put up was none too clean but the best the town afforded. Peter Ilich lay wakeful for hours listening to the noisy songs of some roisterers in the taproom. The lustiness and high good humor of those songs remained long in his memory. When he became a composer he caught the spirit of them in the famous "Drinking Song," Opus 25, No. 6.

Much of the last part of the trip lay through flat, drab country, where only the dismal homes of peasant farmers and little groves of birches and oak trees broke the monotony. It was a thoroughly tired family which arrived at last in the city of Moscow.

Almost an hour before they reached the vast city of the steppes, Moscow's gilded domes and fantastic church spires could be seen glistening in the morning sun. This was the great city formed under the Mongol yoke, the city where the dynasty of Moscow princes grew at last strong enough to defy the Tatar. Once the city took root, dominating the wide steppe with its churches and kremlin high on a hill above the Moskva River, nothing, it seems, could destroy it. In 1237, the Tatars succeeded in burning it, but it rose from its ashes like the legendary Phoenix. By 1520 there were forty-five thousand homes, built of wood. In 1547 most of these houses were destroyed by fire. The city built itself up again. More devastating fires leveled the wooden city—in 1648, 1712, and 1737. Napoleon came to attack the city in 1812, and again proud Moscow burned to the ground. This time the flames had been set deliberately, and by the Muscovites themselves, who by their resolute act defeated the "Grand Army" of the French dictator.

The children felt bewildered and a little afraid. Moscow seemed too big to be real, too busy, too taken up with its own pleasures and worries to give heed to the family of the Mining Inspector from Votkinsk. Troikas dashed through the streets in reckless fashion, their drivers paying no attention to the pedestrians trying to cross the broad thoroughfares. Smaller carriages rolled by more sedately. There were crowds of people buying newspapers at the little corner *kiosks* (shelters), and everywhere vendors of flowers, breads, and *bublichki* (pretzels strung on a stick) cried their wares in high whining tones. Beggars there were in plenty, too, shuffling along as they sang for alms, or standing with outstretched palms, silent.

Peter caught the odd notes of a song sung by a ragged boy of twelve or so selling *bublichki*:

> "I'm just a poor vendor selling my bublichki,
>   Walking all day, hoping someone will buy;
>   Thousands of feet I see, passing the street by me;
>   I raise my voice and cry: 'Bublichki! Buy!' "

Clerks in correct tailed coats and high stiff collars rubbed shoulders with bearded *muzhiks* in sheepskin coats and monks in long black robes. Nuns in their curious conical caps shaped something like the domes of the half-oriental churches moved quietly along in couples and whispered together.

There was a strange uneasiness in the air in Moscow. The Tchaikovskys did not speak of it, but their spirits were damped nevertheless, and their first night in the great city was filled with dismal forebodings.

There was reason enough for Moscow's inquietude. Even Russia, which seemed determined to turn its back on the affairs of Europe and the rest of the world, could not escape the events of 1848 and the years preceding. Earthquakes were shaking the rest of the world even more fiercely than they had during the French Revolution.

The flood of machines had washed over the boundaries of the countries where they originated. England, particularly, felt the need to expand, and this urge brought her into conflict with far-off China, which refused to open its ports for British trade. The Chinese objected particularly to the bringing in of opium from India. There followed the Opium War, 1839-1842, and the mandarins of China were forced to open their harbors to the opium traffic and to other trade as well.

In 1845-6, there was a terrible famine in Ireland. Rather than repeal the Corn Laws, which subsidized the rich landed gentry at the expense of the poor, the rulers of Great Britain let the Irish starve in the streets. In 1848 the wrath of a desperate people joined with the indignation of the world to force repeal.

Gold was discovered at Sutter's Mill at Sacramento in California in the United States. People who had not yet recovered from the financial panic of 1837 begged, borrowed, or stole the money to buy a covered wagon, some beans and flour, and a banjo perhaps to twang out "Oh, Susanna," and the historic trek to the goldfields began. Emigrants from troubled Europe heard about the mines and started their voyages across the Atlantic and around the Horn to join the rush.

In 1848 all the peoples of Europe were muttering ominously, restive under the yoke imposed by the policies of Prince Metternich of Austria, who had dominated Europe since 1815 with his hatred of everything democratic and liberal. France was the most turbulent spot. In 1830 the shopkeepers and merchant traders had supported a revolution which placed Louis Philippe on the throne. In 1848, the monarchy was forcibly overthrown and the Second French Republic established. In Italy, too, and in Austria and Germany people were demanding more freedom. And in that year of 1848, Karl Marx and Friedrich Engels wrote the *Communist Manifesto*, a small pamphlet which set forth the aims of the radical elements in society, a pamphlet which certain men in uneasy Tsarist Russia began to study. Within seventy-five years this study was to produce world-shaking results.

The year 1848 was one of expanding freedom. Metternich and his gang resigned. Other dictators fled from the wrath of their subjects. But the new freedom was merely a lull before the storm. The tyrants were gathering their forces, to crush the people more ruthlessly than ever. Trouble was in the air like a subtle poison.

Small wonder, then, that the Tchaikovsky family were bewildered by the breathless excitement around them. Tired, worried about the future, Mother Alexandra lost some of her usual calm confidence. "Somehow I am afraid for us, Ilya."

"Now, now, my dear. You are tired. Let us get our rest. Morning is wiser than evening." Father Ilya quoted a familiar Russian proverb, and patted his wife's hand kindly.

Lo! the woe - ful night had passed;

6

Next day, Peter, Nicholas, and Sasha stared in wonder at the busy life of the streets. Carriages drawn by brisk horses rolled along the broad avenues, and in front of every hotel were the low narrow vehicles called *droshkies,* lined up for hire. The horses that pulled these little "cabs" were hitched with the characteristic Russian *duga* (yoke). The drivers seemed amazingly out of place in their small rigs. They were swathed in the traditional blue coats which reached to the ground and which were padded out so that one would think the wearers weighed two hundred pounds each.

"One pays these fellows according to their circumference," Father Ilya laughingly remarked as he and his family prepared to hire two of the cabs to take them from the hotel to more modest lodgings. "The more padding, the higher the price. Let's see if we can find two rather thin-looking drivers. We have to begin to think about saving our money, until we are settled again."

Peter took his father's bantering talk about finding a thin

driver very seriously, and was quite distressed when he found
no driver who did not look like an inflated balloon.

When the family was finally settled in temporary quarters,
Father Ilya went to apply for the job he hoped for. Fanny
Dürbach prepared to say good-by. She was leaving the
family, to take another position in St. Petersburg. Before she
left, however, she took the children to see the sights of Moscow. Peter walked until his legs ached, but he was too proud
to complain before the others.

"Moscow is laid out like a gigantic wheel," explained Mademoiselle Dürbach. "The great Kremlin that we see there on
the hill is the hub. Boulevards like Petrovka, Tverskaya, and
Varvarka are the spokes. The walls of the old town form the
first circle; the curving boulevards the second; and the chain
of monasteries the third.

"The princes of Moscow, who planned to defy the Tatars,
laid out the city in this fashion for purposes of defense. The
monasteries were all fortified. From their towers and battle-
ments, soldiers and soldier-monks fought off invaders as long
as possible. If the enemy broke through this line, the defenders retired to the old town, and fought there from the
wall towers. If the besieging forces were still too strong, the
defenders made a last-ditch stand within the walls of the
Kremlin proper."

The children visited the walled city of the Kremlin, entering into the huge square through the Resurrection Gate.
Hundreds of pigeons made a murmurous cooing, feeding un-
molested by the people crossing the square in every direction.
Zinaïda, Nicholas, and Peter stood looking in awe at the remarkable church of St. Basil's, directly opposite the gate.
Every color of the sunset seemed to be blended on the curious
"pineapple" domes with their odd diagonal stripes. Yellow,

red, red-orange, violet, silver, and gilt. Fanny told them that this fantastic church was named, appropriately enough, for a half-crazy begging monk, who wandered in heavy chains all over Russia three hundred years before.

The day was somewhat marred by the sight of the beggars clustered around the entrance of every church and standing under the ikons (pictures of saints) adorning the arches of the arcade along the Kremlin Square. They shuffled along with deformed feet, or dragged paralyzed bodies along the pavements. They displayed repulsive sores or called attention to withered arms. One sightless old man sang a song with words servile and cringing, for some reason repulsive, like the whole miserable system of beggary tolerated in Tsarist Russia. The tune was oddly charming by contrast with the words.

The Beggar's Blessing

May the Lord be kind to you,
You and all your ancestors,
Both your fathers and dear mothers
Grandfathers and grandmothers,
Aunts, uncles, and first cousins.

The evening Fanny said good-by to the family was a sad one for them all. The governess had been with them for four years. To Peter she had seemed like a second mother, and he wept quietly to himself as the carriage taking her away disappeared in the evening shadows.

Mother and Father were gloomy too. Mother's fears about confiding the plans concerning the hoped-for job had been well founded. One of the "good friends" who had listened to these plans in Votkinsk had hurried ahead of the Tchaikovskys and had secured the job for himself.

It was not a small matter to be left without work in a city like Moscow, particularly if there was a large family to be cared for. Father Ilya hurried about to interview other firms, returned home in the evenings tired and discouraged. Mother wrote letters to relatives in St. Petersburg and called on acquaintances in Moscow. The children were left in the care of Zinaïda, who was young and inexperienced, and entirely too impatient and sharp to be either a good teacher or a satisfactory nurse.

Peter, grieving for Mademoiselle Dürbach, denied all opportunity for the time being of expressing his emotions in music, cooped up in stuffy rooms with his irritable brothers and sisters, learned what it meant to suffer frustration and boredom. The child who had won all hearts with his bright smile and gentle ways turned overnight into a short-tempered boy, impolite to his mother and father, unkind in his speech to the other children. No one was more disgusted with his behavior than Peter Ilich himself, but he was unable to mend his ways.

In November, the family left Moscow and went to St. Petersburg. Life brightened for them immediately. Father's brother, the Uncle Peter for whom Peter Ilich was named, and Mother's brother and sister, Mikhail and Yekaterina, were on hand to welcome the family from the Urals. A house was rented on the Vassily Ostrov, near the Exchange, and Peter and Nicholas were sent to school. They settled down to live modestly on their savings until Father Ilya should be able to get another appointment.

The school which Peter and his brother attended was a boarding-school for boys. The Tchaikovsky boys were enrolled as day pupils and allowed to return home at night. Even so, most of their time was spent in the gloomy classrooms. They left home at five o'clock in the morning, long before the winter sun began to warm the dreary streets. Often they did not return to their home on Vassily Ostrov until after five in the evening, and at that time the lamps had been burning for hours. St. Petersburg, which lies even farther

north than Moscow, has colder and gloomier winters than the
city of the steppes. Whereas in summer, the days are nine-
teen hours long, in winter they are woefully short. For two
months of the year the days have almost no sunlight at all.

Blinof's and Mademoiselle Dürbach's tutelage had not
prepared the boys for all the studies of the school. Consequently, they had to do extra work to keep up with their
classes. Often Peter Ilich's tired head was bent over his books
under a flickering oil lamp as late as twelve o'clock at night.

They had a harsh, unsympathetic teacher at school. Peter,
whom Fanny Dürbach had called "brittle as porcelain,"
many times blinked back the tears when he was scolded
roughly. Some of the rowdy boys who lived at the school
noticed his distress and teased him about it. Often he was
forced to fight his tormentors, and on these occasions he returned home scuffed and bruised and sore at heart.

Mother, for all her goodness, did not always see into her
young son's troubles. His greatest consolation came from the
hours he stole, principally on Sundays, to play the piano. The
family bowed to the inevitable, and allowed him to take lessons with the pianist Philipov, though goodness knows when
young Peter found time to study and practice; for his days
were spent in school and his evenings were filled with exciting events—visits from relatives, trips to the theater with his
parents.

In the 1840's people paid little attention to the needs of
growing young bodies. Peter, always inclined to be frail,
broke down under the load that he was forced to carry. He
and Nicholas fell ill of measles in December. Peter's collapse
was complete. For a long time the doctors thought he was
suffering from some spinal trouble. All work, including music
study, was forbidden. Ill, fretful, unhappy, bored, Peter Ilich
had to rest until June of the next year.

Early in the year of 1849 Father Ilya received an appointment to take charge of a factory in the little town of Alapaiev.
Here Peter's only tutor for a while was Zinaïda. He made no
progress with his studies, and was constantly being compared
to his own disadvantage with Brother Nicholas, who had been
left at the school in St. Petersburg. These unkind compari-
sons left a scar which never healed. Peter began to resent
Nicholas' progress, his health, his practical common sense.
Never afterward were these two brothers very congenial.

Peter's mother, writing to Mademoiselle Dürbach, complained: "Pierre is not himself. He has grown idle, learns
nothing, and often makes me cry with vexation."

Finally a new governess was engaged—Natasia Petrov. She
was kind and capable, and Peter began to study conscientiously once more.

About this time, too, he was cheered by the arrival of twin
brothers in the Tchaikovsky household--Anatol and Modeste,
born at Alapaiev in 1850, when Peter was ten years old. It
was like Peter Ilich to want to share his happiness with a
good friend. He took up his pen and wrote Mademoiselle
Dürbach:

"Dear, good Miss Fanny,— It is with great joy I hear the
news of your having so good and industrious a pupil. I want
also to give you some news, my dear Fanny, which may please
you a little; it is of the birth of my twin brothers (on the night
of May 1st) . I have already seen them several times, but each
time I think they are angels descended to earth."

Wind is blow-ing, trees are bow-ing, wild the stormy breezes blow.

7

The cold wind from the Baltic blew streamers of uncomfortable fog through the streets of St. Petersburg. It was early spring in the year 1852, and the muddy streets of the capital city of the "Tsars of all the Russias" kept all but the most venturesome of the pedestrians indoors. A few carriages lumbered behind steaming horses which slipped and struggled through the mud, their flanks plastered with the wet, sticky earth. An unwholesome stench from the marshes accompanied the fog and mingled with the even more disgusting stench of refuse thrown with casual disregard for order or hygiene into the alleys and thoroughfares.

On one of the bleak, forbidding streets of the Baltic city, beyond a gate where an old dog stood guard, a gloomy enough house presented curtained windows to the fog and cold. Like all the homes of the respectable upper-middle-class sort, it offered a dark, cheerless exterior to the world. And even within, the great hall was all dark panels, lighted dimly toward evening by one small oil lamp. The drawing-room was dark and heavy, too, with massive furniture arranged for use rather than show. The room was much too warm, heated as it was night and day by a huge stove.

What was lacking in cheerfulness in the decorations and furnishings, however, was made up by the bright, happy laughter of the group which inhabited it. For this was the Tchaikovsky family, all reunited at last.

The years between 1850 and 1852 had been anything but happy ones for Peter Ilich. At Alapaiev he had made some progress under the tutelage of the new governess, it is true, but Mother Alexandra felt that at ten years of age he should be learning how to study and play with boys his own age. In August of 1850, therefore, she and Zinaïda and Peter had gone to St. Petersburg to make arrangements.

Nicholas was already following in his father's footsteps, attending the School of Mining Engineers. The original plan for Peter had been to send him to the same school, but a long talk with M. A. Vakar, old friend of the family at whose home Nicholas had been living, convinced Mother Alexandra that the School of Jurisprudence would be better for her Pierre. Vakar's brother Plato, a brilliant lawyer with a promising future, was an example held up for Peter to emulate.

So Peter had been left with the Vakars. Mother stayed in the city until October, seeing to it that he made a satisfactory start with his studies in the preparatory division of the law school.

No one, perhaps not even Peter Ilich himself, was prepared for the emotional scene at Mother Alexandra's departure for Alapaiev. Peter, who had never been away from home in his life, suddenly felt that he could not bear to see his mother leave. He broke down and wept and would not be consoled. He begged his mother either to stay with him or to take him home.

"But Pierre, you are a big boy!" she told him. "And you must learn something. You cannot stay in a nursery all your life. You must act like a man, Peter Ilich!"

Peter tried very hard to act like a man, but the tears kept coursing down his cheeks. When at last his mother's carriage was ready to start, he clung frantically to one of the wheels. When the carriage rolled away, he ran after it wildly, hardly knowing what he did. This desperate scene was never erased from Peter Ilich's mind. Even when he was a man, the memory of it could make him wince with pain.

Gradually the terrible homesickness left him, and he settled down to his studies. Life had just begun to fall into a cheerful routine when scarlet fever broke out in Peter's school. The school closed. Peter did not catch the disease, but he carried its germs home with him. His dearest friend, eldest son of the Vakar household, came down with the fever and died. This was the second darkest hour of Peter's childhood. The wound caused by the temporary loss of his mother and home had hardly healed before this new wound was made. Peter blamed himself bitterly as the indirect cause of his friend's death, and the sight of the Vakars' grief crushed his sensitive spirit.

The Vakars moved away from St. Petersburg, and both Nicholas and Peter went to live first with the family of M. Weiss, and then with Plato Vakar. This new home at Plato's was cheerful and friendly. Peter's spirits brightened, and very soon he had learned, just like any other boy away at school, to rely on himself.

In 1852, Father Ilya was retired on a comfortable government pension. Able at last to live wherever he chose, he and mother, Zinaïda and the twins left Alapaiev joyously in the spring to return to St. Petersburg where on Sundays, at least,

Nicholas and Peter could leave school and be with the rest of the family.

Peter was no longer a child, but a tall, slender boy, now always neatly dressed in schoolboy's uniform with collar stiff with official-looking braid. His mop of curly dark hair was as unruly as ever, however, and his remarkable blue eyes had lost none of their wistful charm.

Peter's father and mother cast anxious glances at him on this particular Sunday; for he was listening with rapt expression to the old orchestrion, beloved companion of his babyhood. His parents were not at all pleased that Peter inclined so markedly toward music. Like Fanny Dürbach, they knew all too well the insecurity of life for a musician in the Russia of their day, where music was considered either the plaything of the rich or miserable bread-and-butter for gypsy orchestras.

Peter was unaware of the concerned glances. He was completely absorbed in the gay "Zerlina's Air." This was the music which had first caught his childish attention. It long remained for him the standard of perfect beauty, and all other music was judged by the standard of Mozart.

Tchaikovsky the composer felt that he could never give enough credit to the influence of the great artist from Salzburg. He once wrote: "The music of *Don Giovanni* was the first to make a deep impression upon me. It awoke a spiritual ecstasy which was afterwards to bear fruit. By its help I penetrated into that world of artistic beauty where only great genius abides. It is due to Mozart that I devoted my life to music. He gave the first impulse to my efforts, and made me love it above all else in the world."

The orchestrion was bringing "Zerlina's Air" to a close when a carriage drew up before the house. In a moment Aunt Yekaterina, Madame E. A. Alexeiev, his mother's sister, swept in with that air of hearty good nature which made her a favorite with the family.

"I have it, Petrushka. Just as I thought!" She waved a sheaf of music pages dramatically above her head. "The score of Mozart's *Don Giovanni*. Now you and I shall practice singing the whole opera, soprano, contralto, bass, and tenor parts, all!"

Peter's eyes sparkled. His father and mother with characteristic good nature and solicitude for a favorite son's happiness settled back to listen. They might believe that he was "wasting his time" listening to Mozart on the orchestrion, but they took pride in the facility with which he mastered the difficult parts of the arias of the score brought by his aunt.

Though Peter's immediate family were totally unmusical, they delighted in the light-hearted atmosphere which music and musicians brought into the household. They encouraged the amateur performances of instrumental and vocal music at the parties given to celebrate birthdays and other anniversaries.

At the more festive gatherings, when the guests were many and hearty and the dancing and eating went forward lustily, young Peter Ilich was usually a delighted onlooker rather than a participant. His shyness kept him in quiet corners, where he watched with amusement the antics of the others. This was the role Peter Ilich Tchaikovsky was to play all his life. He watched people around him, translated their happiness and their sorrow into poignant music which at its best is pure emotion.

I have lost my long - be - lov - ed,

8

It was March in the year 1854. In two short months Peter Ilich would be fourteen years old. He was no longer a timid child, but a confident schoolboy, quite capable of looking after himself on his rambles about the city of St. Petersburg and out into the country.

He had come to know and love the cold city which had been built by order of Peter the Great, the city which in 1700 had been a dreary, marshy waste, inhabited only by a few Finnish fishermen. Peter had visited the crude log hut on an island in the Neva, where the hardworking, ambitious, ruthless Tsar Peter had lived when he helped build his "window to the West."

Peter Ilich knew most of the shops which lined the four-mile-long Nevsky Prospekt, had attended the colorful Greek services at the Cathedral of St. Isaak. He had visited the Cathedral of Saints Peter and Paul, where the Russian rulers were buried, but had purposely avoided the Peter-Paul For-

tress next to the Cathedral, tomb of the living, a place of suffering and death for political prisoners.

With the humble side of life in the city the boy deeply sympathized. Among his acquaintances were ragged tellers of tales and singers of folk-songs in the market places. He was friend to old crones selling the huge Russian radishes in the market, peddlers with wares from the bazaars, street gamins with concertinas or balalaikas singing and playing for pennies on church steps.

Long country roads lined with silver birches. The deep muffling snow under a bitter sky at night. The ringing of cathedral bells on frosty mornings. Solemn liturgical masses of the Greek Orthodox Church. Trees along the Nevsky Prospekt in bud in early spring. Lumber barges tied up at old wharves along the Neva. Cossacks making a noisy din with songs of the Don. Fishermen from the Volga singing the melancholy songs of the steppes. These things were truly Russian; something of their beauty and wildness was caught by the composer Tchaikovsky and translated into his music.

Complete master of the Western forms of music and scorning to follow the lead of the fanatic Russian nationalists, who rejected the traditional forms in music, Tchaikovsky nevertheless drew much of his inspiration from national sources. Through him the Western world might hear and understand the country which looked also to the East.

Peter was returning slowly one brisk afternoon from a walk along country roads where the birch trees stood in friendly little clusters, bare yet of leaves, but showing by their sleek bark that the sap was beginning to rise. Darkness overtook him on the way home, but the stars and moon came out to light his path, and the distant sound of church bells made him pleasantly aware that the world of people was within comfortable walking distance.

"What a jolly season spring is," he was thinking. "Full of hope. Everyone and everything seems to be waiting for some miracle. It is like the moment before the concert begins or the theater curtain rises. One cannot escape the feeling that something tremendous is about to happen."

As he walked through the cold night, Peter sang snatches of song—things remembered from the ballet or concert, a stirring march from Glinka's *A Life for the Tsar*, Russia's first opera making use of distinctly Russian folk music. Peter also sang a little folk-song he had learned in Votkinsk, about the tree best loved by the Russians, the silver-barked, fringed-leafed birch tree. (See the next page.)

He fell in step with an old peddler making his plodding way toward St. Petersburg. The peddler's sack hung limp over his shoulder, but it would bulge hugely when the old fellow left the bazaars of Guest's Court on the Nevsky Prospekt. In this one buiding, which housed several hundred shops, the peddler would find all that he needed to sell during the summer in the villages—laces and pins, kerchiefs and gloves, scores of cheap knickknacks for barefooted peasant girls who dared not dream of a trip to the great city.

Peter parted from his peddler acquaintance on the outskirts of town and hurried through winding, crooked streets toward home. The city was throwing off its afternoon sloth and beginning to move about with that oddly energetic manner which urban Russians seem to discover with nightfall.

THE BIRCH TREE

Lit - tle birch-tree grow-ing in the mea - dow,
Cur - ly - leaved and grow-ing in the mea - dow,
Liu — lee, liu-lee, in the mea - dow,
Liu — lee, liu-lee, in the mea - dow.

Richly dressed women and girls fluttered like evening moths toward the warm, well-lighted restaurants, and night owls in capes and silk hats lined up at the *hors d'oeuvre* counters to eat caviar, smoked fish, cheese, and salads, washed down with the inevitable vodka.

Outside, in the raw night, hungry people cast brief glances at all this merriment and went on their way, hopeless, resigned, or rebellious according to their natures. Inside, at the candle-lit tables, fine silver rattled against expensive china, and dainty wine glasses tinkled or were broken after a toast. Nothing mattered to the well-to-do except to let nothing matter.

And yet the volcano was rumbling. Thousands of political prisoners in the damp dungeons of the Peter-Paul Fortress, or chained together for the killing walk to the prison camps of Siberia, were evidence of the will to challenge a government which allowed thousands of peasants in Siberia and the great Volga valley to die of starvation, which stubbornly refused even the wealthy merchant class the right to vote or sit at the council table with the Tsar's noble advisers, which arrogantly asserted that the Tsar received his power direct from God.

Tsar Nicholas I broke under the strain of his fear of his own people. In February of that year of 1854, the Tsar had deliberately exposed himself to extreme cold and thus was able to kill himself without the scandal of suicide by direct means.

Nicholas' son, Alexander, became Tsar as Alexander II. He looked about him and was terrified to observe that the Man with the Hoe was beginning to lift his head and look about him with eyes terrible for oppressors to see. And, as if this were not enough, Alexander found himself in March at war with both England and France in the Crimea.

The world seemed suddenly to have gone topsy-turvy. Louis Napoleon had succeeded in getting himself elected president of France. Then, four years later, at the end of 1851 when another election was coming, he suddenly put through what is known as the *coup d'état*—a piece of political sleight-of-hand that in 1852 made him Emperor; and the Second Republic was no more. Metternich and the Old Guard showed their heads again. And Russia was at war—a senseless war, which built three cemeteries below Sevastopol for the bewildered young soldiers of England, France, and Russia; a war in which a whisky-and-soda-drinking British General gave the wrong order and sent the gallant "six hundred" to their terrible fate in the Valley of Death; a war in which Florence Nightingale and her gallant band of nurses achieved renown in tending the maimed and mutilated British soldiers.

All this touched Peter Ilich very slightly. He would not have realized that Russia was at war if it had not been for the soldiers in the streets and the sound of marching feet at night or the call of bugles. Yet, being sensitive to life around him, he could not escape the uneasiness that prevailed.

A new song died on his lips as he entered a street lined with the meaner types of houses. A woman had screamed out in the quiet night, and a man had laughed coarsely. Peter would not have been Russian if he had not known what this meant. Somewhere a wife was dutifully taking the blows her husband had for her; for in the sad land of the Tsars a whip laid over the shoulders of a wife was considered no more serious a matter than drinking a cup of tea. At peasant weddings, the bride presented her husband with a lash made with her own hands as a symbol of her willingness to take punishment at his hands.

Quiet sobbing more terrible than the cry sent Peter shivering like a beaten puppy out of the street. As he neared the house of his parents, his happy mood had faded and he was hagridden by vague feelings of sorrow.

In later years Tchaikovsky wrote his brother Modeste concerning these sudden seizures of melancholy in the midst of happiness. Like many another artist, the composer steadfastly closed his eyes to the real cause of his suffering and blamed himself or decided that the real reason for his distress could not be discovered.

"Everything," he wrote, "has tended to make today go pleasantly, and yet I am so depressed, and have suffered so intensely, that I might envy any beggar in the street. It all lies in the fact that life is impossible for me except in the country or abroad. Why this is so, God knows—but I am on the verge of insanity.

"This indefinable, horrible, torturing malady, which declares itself in the fact that I cannot live a day, or an hour, in either of the Russian capitals without suffering, will perhaps be explained to me in some better world. . . . I often think that all my discontent springs from my own egoism, because I cannot sacrifice myself for others. . . . The devil knows!"

And yet at another time, he stumbled on a partial truth when he said:

"My nerves are poor, but this cannot be helped. . . . Whose nerves are not disordered in our generation—especially among artists?"

He was a child of his time, unusually sensitive to conditions around him. And his generation lived in troubled days, beset on all sides with the ugly sight of hunger, disease, war, tyranny, and injustice.

Once inside the warm house, with the samovar steaming pleasantly on the round table in the dining-room, with the twins, sturdy boys of four now, making a familiar uproar, Peter felt less unhappy. He turned immediately to the piano to work off his gloomy feelings. Father Ilya looked up with a frown of concern as Peter improvised disturbingly sad melodies. Mother shook her head at the sound of the minor chords. What made the child so moody? she wondered. She could not know that a tortured cry in a poor street at night rang out again in the passionate chords of Peter's improvisation.

In April the Tchaikovsky household was made festive by the marriage of Zinaïda. Her husband was a young engineer, who was planning to take his bride with him to the Ural Mountains. All the relatives and friends in St. Petersburg came to make merry at the wedding supper. Peter forgave

Zinaïda her sharp tongue and impatient ways, and himself played the traditional old marriage song:

THE BELLS OF NOVGOROD

Over the Town of Novgorod
Loud rang the bells . . .

News from the Crimean front was increasingly alarming, and father Ilya shook his head doubtfully when he read the papers. The peasants and poor serfs everywhere in Russia were being forced to add more water to their cabbage soup. Food was being confiscated for the army. There were more beggars in the cities than ever, and more unkempt children trained in the arts of thievery by criminal masters.

Summer arrived, with the hot sun raising a stench from garbage dumps and refuse-strewn streets. The water was polluted everywhere. To drink a glass of it from the tap was to seal one's death warrant. On the warmest days, samovars boiled the poisonous water to provide germ-free tea.

Despite precautions, Peter's mother fell ill of the dread Asiatic cholera. Sitting in dumb misery outside of the door of her bedroom, Peter waited long anxious hours for the doctors to give the family news.

"The crisis is past," they announced. "She is better."

With a sob, Peter sank back in his chair. The others persuaded him to get some sleep, and he stumbled off to bed. Only the doctors and nurses knew when the second crisis in mother Alexandra's illness arrived. There was no time to call the family before she died.

Two years later Peter Ilich wrote his beloved old governess Fanny Dürbach of this tragic loss: ". . . she was taken from us without even time to bid us good-by," he closed his sorrowful letter.

Most people pass from youth into adult life gradually, without knowing where the line between them was. Some pass at one step, as the result of some deeply emotional experience. So it was with Peter Ilich. Just as that first separation from his mother, when he was put in school, marked the end of his childhood, so the death of his mother marked the end of his boyhood.

It was Peter Ilich Tchaikovsky, a man grown, who returned home from the funeral to the cheerless house with his father and brothers and sister. It was a man grown who heard without flinching the news that his father, who had collapsed immediately on his return home, also had cholera.

Waiting, waiting, fearing the dread news he half expected, Peter wandered into the music-room. His slender fingers touched the keys of the piano. How gaily his mother's hands had danced over those same keys only a few days before her fatal illness. What beautiful hands.

"Such hands there never were before, and never will be again," he once remarked in later life.

Peter was sitting at the piano, head buried in his arms, when his father rallied. When it was quite certain that there would be no unexpected crisis, that father Ilya's wonderful constitution would pull him back into life, Peter Ilich raised his tired head. His trembling fingers touched the keys softly, so as not to disturb the patient. Beautiful, tragic melodies, heart-rending but somehow not despairing formed under his facile fingers. The blinding tears came at last; for Peter Ilich was saying his last tender good-by to his dearly beloved mother.

Doc-u-ments, doc-u-ments so long,——————————————— full of grave import

9

With the loss of beloved mother Alexandra, much of their feeling of well-being was taken from the Tchaikovsky family. Uncertainty and anxiety replaced the former cheerful order. Before the gloomy spell was lifted, many changes came to the household.

Father Ilya could not bear the terrible loneliness of a house where Mother Alexandra no longer greeted guests with her gracious smile and quiet, appropriate words of welcome; where her sudden gay laughter was not heard in the garden, as she watched the twins cut up capers for her amusement; where the lilting waltzes she loved no longer danced from beneath her beautiful strong fingers on the keyboard of the drawing-room piano. Uncle Peter Petrovich, who lived with his family in St. Petersburg, invited the broken old man to share his home. So the boys—Nicholas, Hippolite, Peter, and the twins—were put in various schools, and Sasha was enrolled in an institute for girls.

By 1859, the necessity to work and study had softened their

bitter grief. Father Ilya was more like his old self, smiling and kindly, though his eyes were often shadowed with pain when he thought no one noticed him. Nicholas and Hippolite were engrossed in plans for the future. Nicholas was completely absorbed in his School of Engineering activities. Hippolite, training to be a naval commander, could think of nothing but guns and the sea. It had been five years since Russia lost the Crimean War, but Hippolite still bored the family with his ideas of how Sevastopol could have withstood the siege of French and British guns longer. The twins were too young to be part of the life of their brothers and sister. In these circumstances Peter and Sasha turned to each other for companionship, going together to the theater, to the ballet, to the opera, sharing their common enthusiasm for literature and music.

So it was that in this year of 1859 nineteen-year-old Peter Ilich, by this time holding his first job as clerk in the Ministry of Justice, was playing host to his sister, now a young lady of seventeen, and their Aunt Elizabeth Schober. A gay little scene was being enacted in the crowded foyer of a St. Petersburg theater.

"Wasn't it beautifully tragic?" Sasha's usually pale face was flushed, and her eyes sparkled with excitement.

Peter Ilich nodded agreement. "No one in Russia can sing like Lagroua. And in *Norma*—she is absolutely perfect!"

"Yet she is not a beautiful woman," Elizabeth Schober remarked.

"Beauty! What do we mean by beauty?" flashed Peter Ilich. "An actress with even features—classic chin set at the proper angle with the neck, chiseled nose, and so forth—if she could not act the part of Norma with pathos, with deep feeling for tragedy, how then could we speak of her as beautiful? If she moved about the stage like some gnarled old serf of the Volga going to the village well for water—*núka!*"

"That's it," broke in Sasha, supporting her beloved brother's argument. "That is the secret, I think. To walk about the stage in such a way as to suggest power, personality. To be able to indicate tragic resignation with a lift of the shoulder. To have one's voice express every little shade of emotion. To—"

"Enough! Enough!" Aunt Elizabeth threw up her hands in a gesture of mock surrender. "You have conquered me! I shall agree from this moment that Lagroua is a genius!"

Peter and Sasha laughed good-naturedly, and each grabbed one of Aunt Elizabeth's arms and in a manner hardly dignified hustled her out of the foyer and into the street toward a droshky lined up with many others to solicit after-theater business.

"And don't forget, you promised to take us to a very expensive restaurant!" Sasha teased her brother. "I shall order the most costly dinner, let me warn you, so I hope you have saved a considerable sum out of your salary at the Ministry of Justice."

"Don't worry, little pigeon. Now that I am a man of the world, I think I can be trusted to manage a dinner without mishap."

As he helped Aunt Elizabeth and Sasha into the droshky Peter's eyes rested for a moment approvingly on his sister. A warm fur cape covered the flimsy evening dress she wore, but her dark hair was bared to the winter night. Soft flakes of snow sifted down from the dull sky. Some of these had caught in her hair and lay there like apple blossoms before they melted and formed glistening drops of water in her braids.

"Speaking of beauty," said Peter, as he took his place beside his sister and helped adjust the warm fur lap robe, "Sasha here is developing into a very heartbreaker."

"Sing your own tune," admonished Sasha. "Your tall hand-

some figure causes a few hearts to flutter, I have no doubt!"

"How their mother would have rejoiced this evening!" their aunt was thinking. "What fine young people they are!"

Time had worked its healing magic for Peter and Sasha at last, and their lighter spirits were made lighter still by the fact that the mood of the Russian people was less tense. Following the Crimean War, England and France had had their way at the treaty table at Paris. England had temporarily turned her attention from Europe to India, where in 1857 the Sepoys rebelled against their English conquerors. While this two-year war in India was going on and plans were being made in England to transfer the government of the rich colonial empire of India from the old East India Company to the Crown, Alexander II in Russia was having to loosen the checkrein and give his people more freedom.

Rumblings of discontent before the Crimean War had become thunderous when a suffering people realized that the costly war had brought only ignominious defeat. Rumors reached the Tsar that bands of terrorists plotted to take his life. Fearful every minute of the day and night that these rumors would become fact, Alexander sought to appease the wrath of the people by granting certain reforms. Army recruitment was suspended for three years, and many of the troops were demobilized. Homesick peasant boys returned rejoicing to their native villages, and girls married their sweethearts without the clutching fear at their hearts that soon their husbands would be taken from them to die on some foreign battlefield. The government censorship of books, newspapers, and letters was relaxed. The universities were thrown open to all classes of students. The restrictions of the passport system were relaxed. In short, for ten years the people of Russia were allowed to breathe more freely.

Everywhere, as a matter of fact, the old stand-patters were suffering the shocks of progress. In the United States a man by the name of Abraham Lincoln was debating with Stephen Douglas the question of Negro slavery. That was in 1858; and in the following year a man by the name of John Brown was hanged at Harpers Ferry for attempting to organize a slave revolt against the United States Government.

The black-robed priests of the Greek Orthodox Church still led processions of peasants to the rivers in winter, to attack the devils which the ignorant people believed were causing sickness among the cattle and blight to the crops. Arrived at the water, the priests and people, chanting and praying, sought to drive these devils into the icy river, there to stay for the winter. Even as they performed in the name of Christianity these truly pagan rites before the awed people, some of the clergy were uneasily aware of a book published in 1859 in England, a book which presented a scientific explanation of man's place in the universe, of the laws of the creation, a book destined to shake the foundations of those churches which clung to primitive superstitions and old pagan rites. This book was Darwin's *Origin of Species*, announcing for the first time the theory of evolution.

France was at war with Austria in 1859, and trouble was brewing in Poland. Polish patriots had not ceased striving for national independence since 1832, when their country was forcibly annexed to Russia. But for Russia itself there was a feeling of well-being and hope for the future.

Peter Ilich, always so keenly aware of the moods of the people about him, cast aside his gloomy doubts and devoted himself cheerfully to his studies. At this stage in his career he had no thought but of becoming a good clerk in the Ministry of Justice after his graduation from school; of studying just enough to satisfy school authorities; of working just hard enough to hold his job when he got it; of enjoying himself thoroughly and well in his leisure hours.

With some concern, Peter's father watched his son developing into a good-natured, careless, commonplace government clerk. It was not good for a boy to be so indolent, the kindly old man believed. Peter, it seemed, took nothing more seriously than his efforts to avoid work. A task begun and dropped before it was finished. Duties put off from day to day until they were forgotten altogether. No, it was not good.

Though Ilya Tchaikovsky knew absolutely nothing about music or musicians, he had a growing sense of guilt that his son had not been encouraged to make more of his talent. Peter Ilich had become very reticent about his music, showing his resentment of the indifference of most of his family by playing for them only upon request and then with a poor show of courtesy. Father Ilya had eyes to see, however, and he noticed that whenever Peter thought himself unobserved, he would spend hours at the keyboard, improvising delicate, melancholy airs, which were lost forever the minute they were born, since Peter did not put them on paper. It was Father

Ilya, therefore, who surprised his son by hiring for him one of the best piano teachers in St. Petersburg—Rudolf Kündinger. This event took place the year after Mother Alexandra's death. Kündinger was a good teacher, but must have been tremendously thick-headed where discovery of incipient genius was concerned. He was impressed by his pupil's remarkable improvisations and the boy's instinctive feeling for harmony, it is true. Though Peter was entirely ignorant of the rules governing the composing of music, he was able to correct Kündinger's own compositions for better harmony. When Father Ilya asked Kündinger if Peter should become a professional musician, however, the teacher replied without hesitation that he found no unusual talent in the boy. Years later Kündinger explained, "I had to take into consideration the wretched status of a professional musician in Russia at that time."

In 1858, Ilya Tchaikovsky once more placed his faith in human nature in the wrong hands, and by this mistake lost the savings which, together with the pension, had enabled him to live without working. This loss was not altogether a bad thing for him. He was forced to leave his melancholy thoughts and busy himself with wholesome practical matters. He was fortunate enough to be appointed Director of the Technological Institute of St. Petersburg and went to live in the house that was furnished him. Elizabeth Schober, his sister-in-law, was persuaded to bring her family and take charge of the household. Once more the Tchaikovsky brothers and their sister were united with their father in a comfortable, cheerful home.

Peter Ilich found life good. He had several interesting friends at school: young Apukhtin, who became a celebrated poet, and even at thirteen was recognized as a genius by such men of literature as Fet and Turgeniev. Gerard, who became a famous lawyer. Vladimir Adamov, scholarly, hard-working, fond of music, who after leaving school rose to a high position in the Ministry of Justice.

With Apukhtin, Tchaikovsky discussed literature—the ideas and ideals of Pushkin, Lermontov, Tolstoi, Turgeniev, Dostoyevsky, all the great men of letters who dared defy the censors by writing poetry, novels, and dramas in the spirit of democracy. Apukhtin was sophisticated, cynical, very sure of himself. With this friend, Peter Ilich had to pretend to be worldly-wise.

With Gerard, Peter discussed the school magazine to which they both contributed. It was necessary to assume a practical tone with Gerard.

With Adamov, Peter Ilich could be himself. To this friend he confessed his desire for a musical education, told him of all the vague desires and half-formed ambitions.

These two took long walks in the country together. In summer they lay in the tall grass and watched the lazy clouds drifting with the wind overhead. They gathered mushrooms in the woods, and in the fall they wandered through fields where peasants cut and bound the grain and sang the age-old songs.

> Lo, the harvest ripe
> We have winnowed now—
> *Hi-di! La-do!*

"You know, Vladimir, I believe in my gift for music. I could compose if I had the necessary knowledge." Peter wistfully voiced his yearning.

"Why don't you, Petia? Why don't you?" Vladimir spoke eagerly.

Peter kicked a stone out of his path and sighed. "Why doesn't water run uphill? No, Volodya, there are too many forces opposing my wish. I shall probably end my days as a poor clerk in a dismal government office, making out documents, documents, and more documents in a neat hand."

"I don't think so. No, you are wrong," said Adamov thoughtfully.

These two were to remain friends for many years—until Adamov's death in 1877, in fact. The passing of this dignified, gentle, intelligent companion of his schooldays was a blow from which Peter Ilich did not soon recover.

At home Peter found company less to his liking—relatives who bored him so much that even his ingrained courtesy could not conceal his distaste. A restlessness similar to that which he had experienced as a boy of nine caused him to be impatient with his aunts and brothers, to speak sharply to his father, whom he loved intensely.

Once in a while a musician like the famous singing master Piccioli came to call, and then Peter Ilich was himself again. Piccioli was a vain, opinionated, eccentric man. He dyed his hair to conceal the fact that fifty-odd years had frosted it over. He painted youth on his face. And it was said that he wore a mechanical contraption at the back of his neck to pull the wrinkles smooth. Try as they would, the twins, who were fascinated by this story, could never catch a glimpse of the wrinkle-smoother and had to conclude that the old fellow wore his invention under his collar.

Piccioli was very fond of seventeen-year-old Peter Ilich and tried to convert him to his own views concerning musicians.

"Beethoven!" the Italian would snort. "What are his symphonies? Noise, noise! Barbaric. And Bach? Dull, incomparably dull. His fugues raise blisters on the mind! And your precious Glinka and his *Life for the Tsar?* Trash, my dear fellow. Nothing but trash to catch the popular ear. There are only four composers—Rossini, Bellini, Donizetti, and Verdi!"

Peter Ilich always smiled indulgently at these tirades of the prejudiced old singing master. "Here is a man," he thought to himself, "who must have spit on his atlas of Europe with only Italy covered by his hand!"

In the ordinary affairs of life, Tchaikovsky was likely to be putty in someone else's hands. In all things but music this was so. On that subject his opinions were as granite. No amount of argument or persuasion could turn him from what he liked, what he believed in.

During these years of preparing for a clerkship, Peter tried his hand at composing some waltzes. Of this light dance music he kept no record. He did write down one composition, the undistinguished song "My Genius, My Angel, My Friend." With that florid effusion, Tchaikovsky had the good sense to lay down his pen for a while.

In May, 1859, Peter left school and took up his duties in the Ministry of Justice. That he worked none too neatly and hated his working hours was inevitable. An amusing anecdote has survived the years to show us the typical square peg in a round hole. Peter Ilich was sent one day by his superior to deliver a very important document. Tchaikovsky met a friend on the way and stopped to chat. The friend had but half an ear for the conversation, because he noticed Peter Ilich doing a most extraordinary thing. As Tchaikovsky talked, he nervously bit off the corner of the paper he carried, chewed the fragment, and blew it out of his mouth in order to make room for another bite.

The friend could bear the suspense no longer. "Peter Ilich, before you continue, pray tell me whether that legal-looking document you are chewing has a good taste? The Englishman Bacon once wrote that some books are to be tasted, some to be swallowed whole, some to be chewed and digested—but upon my word this is the first time I have ever seen the advice followed literally."

Peter looked in sudden horror at the paper which he had reduced to a ragged fragment. "*Mon Dieu!*" he exclaimed in Fanny Dürbach's manner. "I have eaten up an important document!"

With his friend's laughter ringing in his ears, he ran back to the office. There was nothing for it but to explain to his superior what had become of the document, and wait for a copy to be prepared. Small wonder that Peter Ilich was slow to advance.

We are joy-ous, hap-py, care-free, joy-ous are we.

10

*I*n 1860, Alexandra married handsome Leo Davydov and went to live on the family estate at Kamenka near Kiev. The departure of gay, charming Sasha left the household of men and boys gloomy for a time. Peter Ilich, deprived of the companionship of his sympathetic sister, finding less and less satisfaction in his work, grew silent and irritable by turns.

His father noticed his son's unhappiness and guessed its cure. At dinner one evening he spoke up abruptly. "It is not too late for you to become an artist, Petia."

If Father Ilya had begun to sing the *Marseillaise* during dessert or had risen to hurl the samovar through the window, Peter Ilich and the rest would not have been more astonished.

"Do you think so?" Peter managed to say almost casually.

"It is all decided. Pick out some teacher. What about that Zaremba I have heard you mention, the teacher of harmony and such mysteries? See him, Petia. I shall make all arrangements."

So it was that the mediocre young clerk became the en-

thusiastic music student, studying thoroughbass (a sort of
musical short-hand) with the famous teacher of theory
Nicholas Zaremba.

As wise old Ilya Tchaikovsky had hoped, a remarkable
change took place in Peter Ilich. He was less irritable at home,
less inclined to bury his feelings of boredom and frustration
in senseless or trivial pleasures. He even began to take notice
of the twins, who were often lonely and somewhat neglected
by a household of adults all of whom had their own interests
and problems.

Modeste has told the story of this happy awakening of an
older brother's love:

"One long and wearisome evening, as we sat on the drawing-room window-sill kicking our heels, Peter came in and
found us. From our earliest infancy he inspired us, not so
much with love as with respect and adoration. A word from
him was like a sacred treasure. He, on the contrary, took no
notice of us; we had no existence for him.

"The mere fact that he was in the house, and that we
could see him, sufficed to distract our dullness and cheer us
up; but great indeed was our astonishment when, instead of
passing us by unobserved as usual, he stopped to say: 'Are you
dull, boys? Would you like to spend the evening with me?'
To this day I cannot forget that memorable evening; memorable indeed for us, since it was the beginning of a new
existence.

"The wisest and most experienced of teachers, the dearest
and tenderest of mothers, could not have replaced Peter Ilich
in our life from that hour; for he was all this, and our friend
and comrade besides."

All the Tchaikovsky relatives and friends, even the twins,
young though they were, began to notice that Peter Ilich was
a changed person. Ambition was stirring in him, giving

sparkle to his eye and energy to his step. Study with Zaremba was paying dividends, his father reflected with satisfaction.

This new interest in life, however, was being viewed a trifle doubtfully by the very young man whose sole artistic interest for years had been music. The truth is, Tchaikovsky was afraid that he had started his study too late in life. He reflected that most important composers and virtuosi were masters of their art in early youth. Mozart had composed minuets at the age of three and four years. And here he, Tchaikovsky, at the age of twenty-one, was to begin practically from the beginning. He confided his doubts to Sasha in a letter: ". . . My talent, supposing I really have any, would hardly develop now."

At this stage, to give up his work in the Ministry of Justice in order to devote all his time to the study of music would have been a laughable idea, not only to his family but to Peter Ilich as well. As a clerk he worked as conscientiously as was possible for one who disliked his occupation. In the evenings he attended Zaremba's classes in much the same spirit in which he and many another young man of the upper middle classes attended study-groups dabbling with Italian. It was quite the thing to do. Tchaikovsky continued to amuse himself with a trivial social life and to take nothing very seriously. His doubts and his hopes concerning music were not confided to anyone.

More important to him at this time than his music was the dream of a trip abroad. The young men of his class took such a trip as a matter of course. Anyone who had not puttered for a few months around Berlin, London, and Paris was hopelessly out of fashion. Nothing could measure Peter Ilich's excitement, therefore, when an old friend of his father's suggested that young Tchaikovsky would be the ideal companion to accompany him on a business tour of the Continent and England. Peter wrote the good news to his sister:

"As you probably have heard already, I am to go abroad. You can imagine my delight. . . . This journey seems to me at times an alluring, unrealizable dream. I shall not believe it until I am actually on the steamer. I—in Paris! In Switzerland! It seems ridiculous to think of it!"

Peter Ilich was to earn his way by acting as interpreter, since he spoke French fluently, German fairly well; had a smattering of English, and a bookish knowledge of Italian.

Before Peter left St. Petersburg, his father insisted that he take an extra sum of money with him to be used in an emergency. For the first time in his life Father Ilya was showing caution where his fellow man was concerned. As matters turned out, this bit of foresight extricated Peter Ilich from an unpleasant situation during his trip.

In July the excited young man and his middle-aged traveling companion set out for cities surrounded by an aura of romance since the days when Fanny Dürbach had instructed her pupils in geography and history while "Pierre" held the atlas.

Berlin was the first stop. It was the custom in Tchaikovsky's day to find nothing good in this capital of Prussia; so Peter Ilich, child of his time, walked along the Unter-den-Linden and saw only those things which made him smile patronizingly or frown with distaste. He visited Kroll's and a dance hall, and attended a performance of Offenbach's *Orphée aux enfers*; whereupon he wrote home smugly: "Now we know our Berlin thoroughly, and have had enough of it!"

The next stop was Hamburg. The good citizens of that important port on the north branch of the River Elbe would no doubt have been flattered had they read that this obscure young man from St. Petersburg found their city "a considerable improvement" over Berlin. Truth to tell, Tchaikovsky was fascinated by the busy docks, where ships of all nations were unloading their cargoes of wool, hides, tobacco, iron, grain, and coffee, and taking on the cargoes for which Hamburg acted as a sort of gigantic exchange—sugar, coffee, woolen and cotton goods, ironware, machinery, tobacco, and paper. And this supercilious, tea-drinking young Russian learned to like the aroma of coffee which hung in the air wherever the green beans were being roasted for export, and to drink cups of the fragrant liquid with his sweet rolls at breakfast.

From Hamburg the travelers went to Ostend. They stayed at this fashionable watering-place on the North Sea for three days, and Tchaikovsky was sorry to leave. "I love the sea," he wrote home, "especially when it foams and roars, and these last days it has been furious."

At Ostend they took ship for London, which they found gloomy from smoke and wet with fog and intermittent drizzles of rain. The huge, sprawling city, with its history written in towers and bridges and churches, fascinated Peter Ilich. What memories of dark secrets and shameful bloody deeds the formidable Tower of London guarded with its grim walls! And the great Thames—what strange dramas had been enacted on its banks, dramas with actors speaking many tongues; for Britons, Celts, Romans, Angles, Saxons, Jutes, Danes, Normans, these and many others had played their parts in the checkered history of the great tidal stream.

London was the city of Charles Dickens, with whose books Tchaikovsky was already familiar in translated form. A few years later Peter Ilich wrote to the twins concerning his fondness for Dickens:

". . . I laugh heartily over Dickens' *Pickwick Papers*, with no one to share my mirth; but sometimes this thought incites me to even wilder hilarity. I recommend you to read this book; when one wants to read fiction it is best to begin with such an author as Dickens. He has much in common with Gogol; the same inimitable and innate humor and the same masterly power of depicting an entire character in a few strokes. But he has not Gogol's depth. . . ."

Everywhere he walked in London Tchaikovsky saw the inns and coaches out of the Dickens stories, the Old Curiosity Shops, the dismal warehouses where children worked long hours, the cold dark schools where schoolmasters were freer of the lash than they were of instruction from books. He saw the same whimsical faces, the queer fat and lean, short and tall, smiling and scowling people that the English author portrayed so sympathetically. Sam Weller and his father, Mrs. Gamp, Mr. Toots, Dick Swiveller, David Copperfield, Mr. Micawber, Mr. Creakle, Scrooge and the Cratchits—somehow they were all there.

Tchaikovsky was quick to discover Elizabethan England, too. Sitting in a quaint old inn, not unlike the *Mermaid* where Shakespeare and Ben Jonson had made the air crackle with their electric wit, Peter Ilich ate Cheshire cheese and drank tea, which the English take a little stronger than the Russians do. Yes, truly, he thought to himself, it would have been a great stupidity if Fanny Dürbach had let him think that Russia held all the wonders of the world.

Days before he was to leave London, in spite of the interesting life he led there, Tchaikovsky was longing to return home. Russia might seem intolerable when he was there, but the moment he stepped across the border he found himself, all the days of his life, homesick for family and friends and familiar scenes. On this trip it was the prospect of visiting Paris which buoyed him up.

Just before he left London, he went to hear celebrated

Adelina Patti, most famous singer of the nineteenth century and one of the greatest of any age. His arrogant youthfulness and naïveté prompted him to write that he could see "nothing particular" in this charming woman with the thrilling voice; in later life, Tchaikovsky gladly reversed this opinion.

Paris was a fitting climax to this first tour abroad. For six weeks Peter Ilich plunged enthusiastically into the pleasures which the gayest of all nineteenth-century capitals had to offer. He sat for hours over a bottle of red wine at a table of one of the little sidewalk cafés. Early in the mornings or in the cool dusk, he wandered along the Grands Boulevards, built upon the ramparts constructed in the fourteenth, sixteenth, and seventeenth centuries. From these boulevards there were fascinating glimpses of the picturesque "old city."

He watched the fishermen along the Seine, lined up with their poles and never a fish to justify their amazing patience. He bought paper-backed editions of famous books in the bookstalls. Strolling along the neat walks of the Jardin des Plantes with its famous collection of plants from all over the world; visiting the Louvre, the garden of the Tuileries, the Bourse, the Palais des Beaux Arts, the Cathedral of Notre Dame; going to the national theaters in the evenings to see the famous classic dramas of Corneille and Molière—from morning till night Peter Ilich gave himself up to pleasure.

Once he caught sight of the famous writers Dumas— father and son. It struck Peter Ilich that the elder man, author of such works as *The Three Musketeers*, was the fanciful child; that the son, author of *Camille*, was the adult and for that reason not quite so winning as his father.

Paris saw the climax of Tchaikovsky's growing dislike of his companion. He became painfully aware that this man whom his trusting father had accepted as friend was a man of gross tastes and unfair turn of mind. Misunderstandings deepened into estrangement, and by mutual consent the two parted. Peter Ilich was fervently thankful for the extra money his father had put into his pocketbook.

He hurried home, glad to return to work and study. Writing to his sister, he was economical to the point of stinginess with his information: "What shall I tell you about my journey? It is better to say nothing. If ever I started on a colossal piece of folly, it was this same trip abroad. . . ."

Then he added a significant postscript: "I have begun to study thoroughbass, and am making good progress. Who knows, perhaps in three years' time you will be hearing my opera and singing my arias."

He wrote this half-joking boast in November 1861. Before a month was out he had changed his bantering to deadly earnest. He wrote Sasha: "I promise you that I shall do something. Luckily it is not yet too late."

The twins meanwhile were discovering that easygoing, pleasure-loving brother Peter could turn his hand to real work if need be. For hours he worked out intricate exercises on paper, and played what Modeste called "abominable fugues and preludes." The younger boys looked at the piano and exercise books rather jealously, for these things were taking up time which otherwise might have been devoted to them.

The pattern of Tchaikovsky's whole life was changing. He gave up his trivial pleasures, dropped some of the devil-may-care friends, stayed at home more. Many evenings found him at the chessboard with Father Ilya, whose delight at having his son's companionship was touching. Serious friends dropped in, and conversations turned to matters important to the Russian people. There was much to discuss. The year 1861 was a momentous one in the land of the Bear. The Tsar had that year to bow to popular demand to bring his country out of the Middle Ages. The Crimean War had borne a little good fruit along with the bad, it seems. At any rate, the temper of an outraged people forced the Tsar to free the serfs in the year of 1861.

The peasantry were to learn that what was given with one hand was taken away with the other. Nevertheless, men were free in Russia at last to move about at will, free to leave the land if they chose to go to the cities. If they were free also to starve, they were likewise free to lift their heads and demand better than starvation.

Peter Ilich was also paying strict attention to his clerk's duties. In the autumn of 1862 he was in line for promotion. Autumn came, however, and another was promoted over Peter's head. Furious, Peter Ilich resolved to sever his connections with the bureaucratic world as soon as possible and devote himself to music altogether.

Brother Nicholas on hearing of this proposal was indignant. "You must be mad, Peter," he asserted. "You have a good job. True, government jobs are not the most interesting ones in the world, but they are steady. And suppose you do become a fair musician. What is there to look forward to? A few miserable teaching assignments. A hand-to-mouth existence! Even if you had the genius of a Glinka—which I very much doubt—your lot would still be a miserable one. Remember, Glinka could afford to write music. He was a wealthy man."

Peter made no reply to this tirade for some minutes. As Nicholas was preparing to leave the house, however, his younger brother looked up with hurt, defiant eyes.

"Perhaps I shall not turn out a Glinka," he said, his voice shaking to betray his emotion; "but one thing I can assure you—you will be proud some day to own me as a brother."

Nicholas never forgot these words.

For some time rumors had been circulating in St. Petersburg that a conservatory of music was about to be opened under the patronage of the Grand Duchess Helen. When this school was opened and Anton Rubinstein made Director, Peter was among the first who applied for admittance.

No one in Russia or out of it was better fitted than Rubinstein for the tremendous task of organizing a school which would confer on its graduates a diploma and the title Free Artist, thus elevating music to the status of a profession. The great Anton was already a famous figure in Europe, though he was barely thirty-two years old.

Anton Rubinstein's story was an interesting one. He was of Jewish parentage, though in 1830 his entire family had been baptized in the Greek Orthodox Church. This practical step had saved them from persecution at the hand of Tsar Nicholas, who would have sent them into the Jewish Pale, that strip of land lying on the borders of Poland, where Russian Jews were forced to live in sordid ghettos.

Before he was sixteen Anton had mastered the piano under the guidance of his mother and a Russian teacher by the name of Alexander Villoing. Then he was sent to the Conservatory of Paris, where, after a few months' study, it became painfully evident to his teachers that they could learn from him but hardly instruct him. Liszt and Chopin took an interest in the boy and suggested that he go to Berlin to study theory. At the age of sixteen he had completed his studies and established himself as a teacher of music in Vienna.

By the time he was twenty-two Rubinstein had seen his opera *Dimitri Donskoi* acclaimed in St. Petersburg as the work of a master. Six years later he made his phenomenal concert tour of the musical centers of Europe—a sort of triumphal procession, with its climax in London, where he was received with enthusiasm short only of the nearly hysterical reception he was to receive in 1872 in America.

Taciturn in his speech, vital and energetic, supremely capable, keenly intelligent, arrogant, with an Olympian indifference to the fact that though he could make himself understood in a dozen languages he spoke none of them, not even Russian, perfectly. Such was the Director of the Conservatory of St. Petersburg, who looked from under beetling dark brows at the timid applicants for admittance, fired the questions of the entrance examination at them, growled "Pass!" or "Fail!" without looking up.

When in 1862 Tchaikovsky was enrolled as a student in the Conservatory, he kept his job in the Ministry of Justice for the time being. Before many months, however, he could endure no longer the sight of the stuffy offices and stupid documents. Early in 1863 he resigned his position. From this time on Tchaikovsky was never to deviate from his chosen path: the life of the professional musician was his henceforth.

At home many changes had been taking place. Aunt Elizabeth Schober was no longer with the family. Nicholas had received an engineering appointment which took him into the provinces far from the Russian capitals. Hippolite was on a long voyage.

Father and the twins and Peter settled down together to make the best of a bachelor existence. A cook with a large family of children—ten souls in all, the only serfs ever owned by the Tchaikovsky family, and serfs no longer since 1861—tended to their simple wants. She scolded them in motherly fashion if they were late to meals; otherwise, she did not oversee the household very much and left the four Tchaikovskys to their masculine untidiness. In short, everyone was at peace. Peter, who had at last found his life's work, was amazingly happy and industrious.

Song that   that   the   toil - er   sings. ——

II

etween the fall of 1862 and January 1866 Tchaikovsky gave himself up completely to the studies at the Conservatory. The rest of his fair-weather friends dropped away from him; shortly only Adamov and Apukhtin remained.

At school he made new friends. Among them were N. A. Hubert, and the brilliant seventeen-year-old youth, Hermann Laroche, whose father was established in St. Petersburg as a teacher of French. Hermann's mother, an accomplished linguist, had supervised her son's early education, musical instruction being not the least of the boy's advantages. Dubuque, his music teacher, had persuaded young Hermann to give up the idea of becoming a virtuoso, since his hands were not ideally suited for the piano. Instead, he had been encouraged to compose music, and at the age of ten he had to his credit a march and an overture. When he entered the Conservatory in 1862 he was far ahead of his fellow students in musical training. Besides, he was well read in the literature of music—history, biography, and critical essays.

Tchaikovsky was immediately attracted to the younger student, who possessed the typical Gallic wit and liveliness. Very soon they were inseparable companions. Tchaikovsky valued Laroche's critical judgment and his amazing book-learning. Laroche valued the help which Tchaikovsky was able to give him in the personal relationships which at first baffled the boy who had been brought up apart from crowds.

"How do you always know the proper thing to say to everyone?" Laroche would marvel. "I offend everyone by some chance remark or criticism; you can say the same things and no one minds. I dare to say that the full modern orchestra will take the place of the classical orchestra of Mozart or the slightly expanded orchestra of Beethoven—and the great Anton roars at me like a lion. You compose for the modern orchestra—and aside from a grumble or so he seems not to notice."

"I would willingly give up my other 'conquests' to win Anton," sighed Tchaikovsky. "He is a very great man. And he views me very often as something distasteful which nevertheless must be swallowed."

This coldness of Anton Rubinstein always baffled Tchaikovsky. They were friends until they began to talk music; then a wall came between them. The fact was that these two men of genius had widely different talents and tastes. Anton, the great piano virtuoso, was unable to comprehend a young man whose chief talent was composing for orchestra, the full modern orchestra with which Tchaikovsky had become familiar through listening to the works of Berlioz, Liszt, Wagner, and Glinka.

Laroche, who was not slow to recognize Tchaikovsky's docility in the ordinary affairs of life, marveled at his stubbornness in sticking to his musical opinions. "His judgment," wrote Laroche in later years, "was always somewhat skeptical; his need of independence remarkable."

No question about the strength of will and independence of student Tchaikovsky, the penniless, unknown young musician who could study with one of the greatest musicians of Europe—a man of dominating personality and high temper—admire this man and learn from him, yet never once pretend to agree with him in certain musical matters. Arrogant Anton Rubinstein must have raised those bushy dark eyebrows of his and looked at the stubborn student in much the same way as a parent would view a two-year-old who presented a declaration of independence and bill of rights all drawn up in the best legal terms.

In the spring of 1862, Tchaikovsky gave up the detested government position and became a full-time student of the Conservatory. Writing his anxious sister, he explained but did not apologize:

"My musical talent—you cannot deny it—is my only one. This being so, it stands to reason that I ought not to leave this God-sent gift uncultivated and undeveloped. . . . The professors are satisfied with me and say that with the necessary zeal I shall do well. I do not tell you all this in a boastful spirit (it is not my nature), only in order to speak openly to you without any false modesty."

This letter was written shortly before the term closed at the Conservatory. Tchaikovsky spent the summer outside of St. Petersburg, at the country home of his friend Apukhtin. When he returned for the fall term, Tchaikovsky gave outward evidence of the changed inner man. His hair had grown long, since haircuts cost money and money was being hoarded for the precious tuition. A once-fashionable coat hung on his youthful frame in unfashionable folds, and showed signs of fraying at the cuffs.

Father Ilya had moved into modest lodgings, which he shared with his son. The twins were in school and visited their father and brother only on holidays. As for Peter, he gave up all amusements and sat night after night in his bare little room, which held only a bed and a table, and worked out exercises.

During those days Peter Ilich lost the amateurish approach to his art and became the true professional in his respect for honest craftsmanship.

"An artist must work the way a shoemaker does," he often said in later life. "Mozart and Beethoven worked like that."

Tchaikovsky often asserted that he composed in two ways: by inspiration, and "to order." Many of his best short piano works were composed in this latter way, the composer sitting down with only the vaguest idea of what he wanted to write and not getting up until the melody was complete.

The *1812 Overture* was one of the longer compositions that Tchaikovsky wrote to order. It was written in 1880, when the composer was famous enough to turn down a "tailored-to-measure" assignment if he had chosen to do so. On the contrary, Tchaikovsky busied himself cheerfully with the task of writing triumphal music "to order" for the celebration to be held in the great Kremlin Square of Moscow, commemorating the Russian victory over Napoleon sixty-nine years before. The organizers of the celebration planned to have the overture performed by a colossal orchestra. The big drums of the musical score were to be replaced by salvos of artillery electrically controlled from the conductor's podium, and the music representing the actual defeat of the French army was to be accompanied by the ringing of the cathedral bells of the

Kremlin. Fortunately for Tchaikovsky's peace of mind this bizarre performance did not take place.*

The Russian hymn *God Preserve Thy People* opens the overture. Quiet, foreboding passages follow, leading up to the main section, where snatches of Russian folk music are brought into violent conflict with the *Marseillaise* to represent the fateful battle of Borodino. The work ends with the Russian hymn and the jubilant ringing of bells.

The Largo from the *1812 Overture* is the victorious Russian theme:

Igor Grabar, in his autobiography recently published in the Soviet Union, relates a conversation he had with Tchaikovsky on the subject of art and work. Grabar had made the trite remark that men of genius create by inspiration. Tchaikovsky immediately took issue with this remark.

"Young man, don't talk banalities," he said sharply.

"But, Peter Ilich," Grabar protested, much surprised at the seriousness of Tchaikovsky's tone. "If you have no inspiration while composing, then who has it?"

"One must not wait for inspiration to come; inspiration alone is insufficient. What counts before anything else is work, more work, and still more work. Remember, that not

---

* In 1936 a W.P.A. orchestra in New York performed the *1812 Overture* with sixteen rifles and a 10-gauge gun. And in June 1940 the Philadelphia Orchestra, at one of its summer concerts, played it with the two cannon called for in the original score—the first time that this had been done in America.

even a genius can produce anything great, or even mediocre, if he will not work hard. The greater his gifts, the more work is required. I consider myself the most ordinary, mediocre person."

Grabar would not swallow that last statement and tried to protest again, but Tchaikovsky interrupted impatiently:

"No, no, don't argue. I know what I am talking about, and I talk sense. I advise you, young man, to remember it for life: 'inspiration' is born only of labor and in the process of labor. . . ."

With firm faith in this creed of work, which was later to produce such compositions as the *1812 Overture*, Tchaikovsky did not spare himself during his early student days but plunged into the study of piano, harmony, and counterpoint, and orchestration. In this last, his teacher was Rubinstein. Himself a tireless worker, Rubinstein discovered to his amazement that he had met his match in Tchaikovsky. With a kind of sardonic humor he set this student the most formidable tasks, and Peter Ilich's pride refused to let him cry "Enough!"

"Sometimes," Laroche said, "he spent the whole night upon some score he wished to lay before his insatiable teacher on the following day."

During these years Tchaikovsky took in new musical impressions as a sponge takes in sea water and food particles. What he found to his liking he kept and digested; what he did not find good, he cast out.

In 1862 Richard Wagner came to St. Petersburg and conducted a series of concerts to acquaint the Russians with excerpts from his earlier operas and with portions of his *Niebelungen Ring*. Wagner's music failed to stir Tchaikovsky; the orchestration, however, roused in him the liveliest interest.

About this time, too, Tchaikovsky took lessons on the

organ from the famous Heinrich Stiehl. In the hushed twilight of the Lutheran Church in St. Petersburg, the young composer learned the mysteries of the stops and pedals. He was not long attracted by the sonorous melodies of Bach and other writers for the organ, however, and he himself never composed for the organ.

With Laroche he played the piano arrangements of Beethoven's Ninth Symphony (*choral*), Schumann's Third Symphony (*Rhenish*), Wagner's *Lohengrin*. Two Russian works made a profound impression on him: Anton Rubinstein's *Ocean* Symphony and the critic Serov's opera *Judith*. Listening to Henri Litolff's two overtures *Robespierre* and *Les Girondistes*, there was instilled in him a profound liking for program music—music that attempts to tell a story or paint a scene or express a definite thought. Laroche once said: "In his early overtures, including *Romeo and Juliet*, the influence of Litolff is easily perceptible."

As for Liszt, Tchaikovsky detected a certain insincerity in his work. This feeling was later transferred to Liszt himself. In 1879 Tchaikovsky wrote: "He is at heart a good man, one of the very few great artists who have never known envy . . . but he is too much of a hypocrite."

Tchaikovsky's progress at the Conservatory was not unmarred by mishaps. One of the most painful experiences of his schooldays was his first attempt at conducting. The advanced students of composition were expected to conduct the school orchestra in turn. There was no way for Peter Ilich to sidestep this duty, though he suffered agonies of fright at the very thought of displaying his talents before a crowd of people.

Laroche wrote of the event: "He declared that having to stand at the raised desk in front of the orchestra produced such nervous sensations that all the time he felt his head must fall off his shoulders; in order to prevent this catastrophe, he kept his left hand under his chin and conducted with his right only. This fixed idea lasted for years. . . . "In 1868 Tchaikovsky was invited to conduct the dances from his opera *The Voivode* at a charity concert given in Moscow. I still see him before me, the baton in his right hand, while his left firmly supports his fair beard!"

Among those who offered friendship to modest Peter Ilich during the Conservatory days was a Russian prince, Alexis Galitsin, owner of an estate of fabulous magnificence in Kharkov. To this country home of Trostinetz, Tchaikovsky went to spend the summer of 1864. In the most luxurious surroundings, the young composer led a fairy-tale existence.

Prince Galitsin delighted in surprising his musical friend with all sorts of celebrations in his honor. On Tchaikovsky's name-day the Prince ordered a fête. Early church service was followed by a breakfast to which neighbors from far and near rode up in fashionable carriages. The afternoon was spent in conversation and listening to music. In the evening, Galitsin led the way along a path through the woods of ash and oak and birch. Torches flared to light the guests to a tent where a banquet had been laid on long oak trestles.

On the green around the pavilion, folk-dancers had been assembled. Girls and boys in bright embroidered costumes and boots of red leather stamped out the national dances to the music of balalaika and concertina in the soft summer evening. Men with rich voices sang folk-songs, lively ones about "The Snowball Tree," sad, brooding ones like "The Sleeping Lake."

Closing his eyes, Peter Ilich felt with his sensitive fingers along the frayed cuffs of his shabby coat and smiled his gentle but sardonic smile. Could this be the music student who lived on the grand total of fifty rubles (about $25) a month earned by giving piano lessons to pupils drummed up by Rubinstein?

In the midst of all this luxury and entertainment Tchaikovsky insisted that he have a certain number of hours to himself each day, in order to complete a summer exercise set by Anton Rubinstein. Galitsin with a shrug and whimsical smile had to agree.

The exercise set was the composing and orchestrating of an overture to a Russian play, *The Storm*, by Ostrovsky. This was Tchaikovsky's first independent musical work.

The storm is the climax of the story, forming the subject of the last part of this student composition (never published); but it was nothing to the storm of wrath which the piece aroused when the great Anton examined it. As a sort of joke, Tchaikovsky—who knew well enough that his use of such bizarre combinations of instruments in the score as the tuba, English horn, harp, tremolo for violins *divisi*, would be rank heresy in Rubinstein's eyes—sent the work by post to Laroche. That trusting young man followed instructions and took the piece to Rubinstein.

"Never in my life," said Laroche, reporting the experience, "have I listened to such a homily—it was Sunday morning, too!"

Joke or not, this piece of music was Tchaikovsky's first step on the long difficult road to fame, a road which led him eventually upward to the heights.

And my tune flows like sil - ver

12

$\mathcal{P}$eter Ilich returned to St. Petersburg in the fall, cheerfully accepting his poverty-stricken existence. His position was made less drab by the kindly solicitude of some new friends—relatives of the Leo Davydov whom Sasha had married: Alexandra Ivanova Davydov, mother of Leo, widow of the famous "Decembrist" Vassily Davydov, who had suffered a long Siberian exile for his political views, and five of her large family. Two of the daughters, Elizabeth and Vera, became Tchaikovsky's lifelong friends, at whose home he was always welcome when the storms of his life drove him to shelter.

In this year his father married again. His wife, a modest woman without education, kind-hearted and devoted to old Ilya, won Peter Ilich's respect. Good Mother Elizabeth Alexandrov welcomed her stepson whenever he chose to leave his drab little room and spend the evening with his father and her, mended his clothes, cooked his favorite dishes, lent him money. Peter Ilich spoke of her always with the deepest affection.

It was in the summer of 1865 that Tchaikovsky realized a dream of long standing. He and the twins went to stay with their beloved sister Sasha at Kamenka on the banks of the Tiasmin River, near Kiev.

This place was to assume tremendous importance for the composer in later years. It not only represented a haven, where his motherly sister and good-natured brother-in-law and their lively growing family always made him welcome, but also held stirring memories of the romantic past. Here had been hatched the plots of the Decembrists, those revolutionaries among the nobility who had opposed autocratic monarchy and serfdom by organizing a revolt against the government in December 1825. Here the ardent young poet Pushkin, great-grandson of the Negro who was the favorite of Peter the Great, had spent hours in Kamenka's famous grotto, writing verses about his days of exile in the Caucasus, dreaming of the story he was to write about Tatiana and Oniegin.

Mother Alexandra Davydov and her daughters often spent their summers at Kamenka. And in addition to all these, Nicholas Davydov, real owner of Kamenka, puttered about his garden or shut himself away from the world to be with his books. This eldest son of Mother Davydov influenced Tchaikovsky's political views perhaps more than any other person. His arguments convinced the composer that, no matter how mismanaged affairs of state were in Russia, democracy would not be a cure for them.

Had Tchaikovsky continued to give ear to the talk of liberal friends he might have rejoiced in the bravery of the armed guerrilla bands in Poland which in 1863 dared to defy the power of the Tsar. He might have condemned the ruthless ravaging of Polish towns to put down this insurrection. He might have shuddered to think that the same Tsar Alexander II who had made a gesture toward progress in freeing the serfs could act with such savagery in suppressing the Polish language, closing Polish schools, crushing any who championed the idea of a Polish nation.

As it was, Peter Ilich hardly thought about these things, dismissing as a trouble spot a nation which did not want to be Russianized. Certainly he had no way of knowing that in that same sad, war-torn country of Poland an obscure professor was continuing to carry on illegal work by teaching children of Polish parents the Polish language, and that this professor had a daughter whom many years later the world was to acclaim as Madame Curie, with her husband the discoverer of radium.

Tchaikovsky most certainly paid no attention to the Civil War in America. What significance was there for him in the surrender of Lee in April of the year 1865? Or of President Lincoln's assassination a few days later? Art could be separated from the events of the world, from politics and war—so he believed.

He could not escape his environment, of course. Already at Kamenka he began to be disturbed by doubts and an unexplained melancholy. He complained of trifles: The folksongs of "Little Russia" were a disappointment. He had expected to hear every peasant woman in the kitchen and every gardener on the estate singing melodies worth noting down. He declared that he found only one song worth remembering (this despite the fact that in later years he gathered several songs at Kamenka). This folk-tune which he condescended to record was used eventually in his *Scherzo à la russe* for piano, Opus 1, No. 1.

This same summer, Peter completed the orchestration of the "Dances of the Serving Girls," a gay piece he afterward used as ballet music in his opera *The Voivode*. He sketched out a Concert Overture in C minor, and worked hard to complete a task entrusted to him by Anton Rubinstein—the rendering into Russian of Gevaert's French book on instrumentation.

Tchaikovsky had very little money when he said good-by to Kamenka at the end of the summer and returned with the twins to St. Petersburg. He was expecting payment for the translation, however, and intended to resume his teaching.

The trip home was full of adventure of the most unpleasant sort. The horses hitched to the great coach which carried the travelers by post stages toward St. Petersburg shied at some fox or rabbit in the road and ran away. The coach was over-turned, and Tchaikovsky and his brothers crawled out from under it shaken, bruised, and scratched, thankful that their lives had been spared.

Black bread and water was the only food they could procure, the rest of the provisions of the countryside having been commandeered by the Grand Duke Nikolai for his troops. It is highly probable that Tchaikovsky's faith in the autocratic rule of Tsar and princes in Russia was somewhat shaken, at least temporarily, by the starving he and the twins did on this uncomfortable trip.

The streets of St. Petersburg were rivers and the dark buildings sodden and forbidding when the brothers arrived;

for the cold fall rains had set in. When the twins were established once more in their school, Peter Ilich turned with none too happy a heart toward his dismal little room for which he paid eight rubles ($4) a month. Parting with Modeste and Anatol was never a happy task. Anatol usually winked back the tears, but Modeste's lip invariably trembled in a way to make the older brother's heart ache. Peter Ilich on these occasions remembered poignantly his parting with his mother when he had first been left at school.

The eight-ruble room was hardly a cheerful haven. It was small and dark and bare and none too warm or dry. There were many other tenants in the same house, most of them the noisy kind given to late parties in their rooms or to stumbling home at all hours from various taverns and making a clatter on the stairs with their boots. The noise bothered Tchaikovsky more than the other discomforts, and the longer he stayed in this room the more he disliked it.

What was worse, he was in debt for the room for many months back. The total of his obligation was 150 rubles. The money he had expected from Rubinstein for the translation was not immediately forthcoming. His teaching furnished him with barely enough money to buy food. The upshot of this situation was that he had to move. After all, a 150-ruble debt piled up at the rate of only eight rubles a month represented to his landlord a long-term investment in a poor student who showed little evidence of being able to improve his fortunes.

Fanny Dürbach's opposition to the career of professional musician, Kündinger's warnings about the "miserable lot of the professional musician in Russia," brother Nicholas' anger at the younger brother's giving up a secure government position to take up music—all these objections must have been as wormwood to Peter Ilich at this time. He was forced to move not once but again and again—and always for the same reason, lack of money.

Bitterest pill of all was the necessity of going to his new stepmother for a loan. Father Ilya was again in the Urals seeking to better his financial position, and Peter Ilich knew that Mother Elizabeth could ill afford to share her modest savings with her stepson.

Mother Elizabeth, good woman that she was, came to his assistance gladly, and Peter Ilich was sure of being able to keep his head above water until graduation day. A sensitive, proud spirit was receiving wounds from these indignities from which it would never completely recover. There is no doubt that a good deal of Tchaikovsky's later fear of meeting people grew out of his having been so poor at this time in his youth, badly dressed, always in debt or under obligations to others.

When he had sunk to such a state of discouragement that even hope for the future seemed dead, a serious affection of the eyes made it impossible for him to work at his music as he had done. It is no wonder that, when well-meaning friends came to suggest that he give up the music nonsense and take a position as Government Inspector of Meat, the composer very nearly consented.

Modeste wrote in his memoirs: "To the great advantage of all consumers, and to the glory of Russian music, the proposal came to nothing."

Then the tide turned, as it frequently does. Tchaikovsky's friend Apukhtin left St. Petersburg for a few months and allowed Peter Ilich to occupy his rooms. This solved the composer's most pressing financial problem. Artistic encouragement came in the form of public recognition by Johann Strauss, the Waltz King from Vienna, who had been in Pavlovsk during the summer as guest conductor for the concerts there. In one of his programs he included the very gay, very Russian "Dances of the Serving Maids."

All doubts of the future were set at rest when Nicholas Rubinstein, Anton's brother, decided to open a conservatory in Moscow. Nicholas Rubinstein was one of the greatest pianists of his day, as famous in Russia as his brother and just as competent. At Anton's suggestion Tchaikovsky was engaged as Professor of Harmony in the new school. True, there was more honor and glory than money connected with the job, the pay being 50 rubles a month, no more than Peter Ilich earned from giving lessons. "However, as the conservatory grew, the pay of its teachers would grow," Peter Ilich comforted himself.

It is amazing that during the months of wandering from room to room, borrowing money for rent and food, and doctoring his sorely overstrained eyes, Tchaikovsky went right on composing music. A string Quartet in B flat minor (of which only the first movement survives in manuscript) and an overture in F major (also in manuscript), arranged by the composer for full orchestra and conducted by him at one of the school concerts, are evidence of Spartan courage.

In November he began the composition which was required of the senior students for their graduation. This was a cantata for chorus and orchestra, a setting for the *Ode to Joy* by the German poet Schiller. Forty-two years before, this same poem had been set to music by Beethoven for the choral part of his Ninth Symphony.

The great day arrived—January 12, 1866. The conservatory's most brilliant student was expected to appear before an examining board composed of the Directors of the Russian Musical Society, the Board of Examiners of the Conservatory, the Director of the Court Chapel, and the Capellmeisters of the Imperial Opera.

The eminent musicians who were to be present at the examination arrived correctly hatted and gloved, each with cane or official-looking portmanteau. The student they were to examine, however, did not arrive, and could not be found. Tchaikovsky had fought his fear of crowds, his shyness, his feeling that his head might fly off—in short, all the nervous symptoms that had kept him trembling and sleepless during the long night before the graduation day—and this battle he had lost.

His cantata was performed and apparently spoke for itself; for in spite of Anton's thunderous rage at having his pupil run away from the oral examination, the examiners agreed that the student composer should have his diploma and a silver medal besides.

The cantata was received in oddly different ways by various musical authorities. Anton Rubinstein was not satisfied with it, at least not to the extent of allowing it to be performed by the Russian Musical Society.

"There must be many alterations," he growled. "As a student piece, as a thing to get you a medal and a diploma when you yourself were not present to get these things for yourself—it is well enough. But it is not good enough as it stands to be placed beside the works of Rimsky-Korsakov, Balakirev, Christianovich. Work it over—then we shall see!"

Rubinstein was not pleased, and Serov was inclined to "damn with faint praise," but their remarks were benediction compared with the blast of sarcastic criticism loosed by César Cui, writer-spokesman for "The Russian Five." Tchaikovsky had paid too little attention to this group of musicians to suit them. In fact, he got to know them personally only after he had moved from St. Petersburg in 1860. They were founding a "school" of music, a radically Russian school which rejected the established forms of music-writing. Their goal was ultramodern music based on native folk rhythms, melodies, and harmonies. Tchaikovsky, starving himself in order to study the very forms they despised, was hardly a proper candidate for membership in the musical *Kutchka* ("the gang" or "the bunch"), as they called themselves. Tchaikovsky loved Russian folk-music and often drew on it for his inspiration; but he held fast to the view that the best way to translate musical inspiration into musical composition understandable by the world was to make use of the accepted Western forms. Tchaikovsky the artist refused to be an isolationist.

Yet "The Five" were not men to be overlooked. Each was talented, sincerely devoted to the idea of expressing Russian themes in their works. In that aim Tchaikovsky was willing to go along with them. His objection to the *Kutchka* seemed to lie in his distrust of amateurs; for in a sense all of "The Five"—Rimsky-Korsakov, Moussorgsky, Balakirev, Cui, and Borodin—composed as an avocation, not as a vocation.

Rimsky-Korsakov was an officer in the Imperial Navy. His great talent for music kept him dabbling in the art until finally he—the only one of "The Five" to do so—undertook serious study. Such works as *The Golden Cockerel* and his Symphonic Suite *Scheherazade* made his name known to millions of music-lovers. Tchaikovsky was one of the first to appreciate Rimsky-Korsakov's genius and to encourage him to throw aside the dabbler's attitude and make music his profession. He was also quick to perceive that Korsakov was to become what the world has since acclaimed him—"the father of twentieth-century orchestration." In a letter written in 1886, Tchaikovsky with the utter lack of professional jealousy which was characteristic of this honest craftsman spoke words of praise which must have warmed the heart of his fellow composer:

"In conclusion I must add that your 'Spanish Capriccio' is

a *colossal masterpiece of instrumentation*, and you may regard yourself as the greatest master of the present day."

Modeste Moussorgsky irritated Tchaikovsky because of his "roughness" and refusal to develop his native gift. In a letter dated 1878, Tchaikovsky wrote of Moussorgsky:

"His gifts are perhaps the most remarkable of all, but his nature is narrow and he has no aspirations toward self-perfection. He has been too easily led away by the absurd theories of his set and the belief in his own genius. Besides which his nature is not of the finest quality, and he likes what is coarse, unpolished, and ugly."

Yet Tchaikovsky recognized Moussorgsky's "very original talent which flashes now and again." He probably wondered that a military man, a member of the Preobrazhensky Guard, could find the necessary leisure and quiet atmosphere necessary for composing such undeniably good music as that of *A Night on Bald Mountain* and *Pictures at an Exhibition*.

As for Balakirev, Tchaikovsky called him "the greatest personality of the entire circle," "the inventor of all the theories of this remarkable circle which unites so many undeveloped, falsely developed, or prematurely decayed talents." Balakirev was the wealthy member of the group. From earliest childhood he had been supported by the serf system, whereby virtual slaves made the living and performed even the most personal services for the rich land-owners. Talented Balakirev, who might have become a good composer if he had had to work for his living, ended by running away from life itself. As Tchaikovsky put it: "After having proclaimed his agnosticism rather widely, he suddenly became pious! Now he spends all his time in church, fasts, kisses the relics—and does very little else." Balakirev might well have sat for the portrait of Oblomov, as drawn by the great Russian novelist Goncharov —Oblomov the man who spent his life "in dressing-gown and slippers, dividing his time among sleep, food, and day-dreams," who "began by not knowing how to put his stockings on" and ended by "not knowing how to live." (Avrahm Yarmolinsky.)

Cui, who never seemed to run out of venomous remarks in his critical writings in the press whenever a new Tchaikovsky composition was performed in St. Petersburg, was characterized by Tchaikovsky after years of this treatment as a "gifted amateur. His music is not original, but graceful and elegant; it is too coquettish—'made up,' so to speak. At first it pleases, but soon satiates us. That is because Cui's specialty is not music, but fortification, upon which he has to give a number of lectures in the various military schools in St. Petersburg."

Alexander Borodin, Professor of Chemistry at the Academy of Medicine, who by his own admission never found time to compose unless he was in bed with a cold, was in Tchaikovsky's estimation a "very great talent, which has come to nothing for the want of teaching." This man, known today for his Symphony No. 2 in B minor, with its Asiatic melodies and Tatar rhythms, had so little technique that he could not write a bar without assistance, Tchaikovsky once remarked.

For a young composer who was trying earnestly to master the Western forms, it was disappointing to feel that Rubinstein, who represented the German school of Beethoven, considered Tchaikovsky's music too radical, too "formless." The cold attitude of Serov, whose opera *Judith* had excited the young Tchaikovsky's admiration, increased his sense of having failed temporarily. The attack by Cui, speaking for "The Five," irritated him somewhat, for in at least one path he had set his feet alongside theirs, and that was the path toward the developing of the rich Eastern music of their Slavic and Oriental heritage.

It was the old friend of his schooldays who bolstered up sensitive young Tchaikovsky's pride. Laroche's letter heartened Tchaikovsky far beyond any praise by members of his family or unmusical friends would have done, for Tchaikovsky knew that Laroche was not only his good friend but his severest critic as well. What he had to say in his letter of January 11, 1866 proceeded from honest conviction:

". . . I will tell you frankly that I consider yours is the greatest musical talent to which Russia can look in the future. . . . In you I see the greatest—or rather the sole—hope of our musical future. Your own original creations will probably not make their appearance for another five years. But these ripe and classic works will surpass everything we have heard since Glinka. . . ."

He shall serve———————— with   hon - or,

13

*S*now lay deep on the roads to Moscow in January of that year of 1866 when threadbare young Tchaikovsky said goodby to his father and the twins, to Uncle Peter and his family, to Aunt Elizabeth, to the dear friends and relatives by marriage, Vera and Elizabeth and Mother Alexandra Davydov. Tears blinded Peter Ilich's eyes as the Moscow train pulled away from the station and he realized that he would not see the familiar scenes of St. Petersburg for many months nor hear the familiar voices of those dear to him. Departures were always to affect Tchaikovsky thus. Wrenching himself away from surroundings and people he loved, he felt as if he left something of himself behind, something torn violently from him, leaving a wound and a scar.

The feeling of melancholy had deepened into one close to despair by the time his train pulled into the station in Moscow. Like one in a trance he found his baggage. In his long winter coat reaching to the ground and round fur cap he looked much like any other Muscovite, and no one glancing casually at him would have guessed that this young man was making a supreme effort to present a calm face to the world. Only those who knew him well, only those who understood the sadness in his expressive eyes, would have guessed what the effort was costing him. Whatever his internal conflict, it was not Tchaikovsky's habit to make a spectacle of himself before the world, and he always managed to fight out the sternest battles of life within his own soul. ". . . He passed through those heavy hours alone," Modeste once wrote of his brother's repression of his troubles; "those around him observed the change only when it had already taken place, and the dawn of a new life had gladdened his spiritual vision."

It was not surprising, therefore, that Nicholas Rubinstein, who walked the streets of any city in Europe like a conqueror, sure of his place in the world, sure of his talents, sure of his ability to bend others to his will, should notice nothing unusual in the young professor's manner when he greeted him in the Moscow station.

"*Nu, nu!*" Rubinstein raised one of those wicked blond eyebrows for which he was as famous as brother Anton was for his shaggy dark brows and unruly long hair. "So!" We have a Professor of Composition at last! Welcome, Peter Ilich Tchaikovsky. I've a little dinner arranged in my rooms. Some of the teachers from the Conservatory to meet you. Come!"

Peter Ilich, who must have longed for nothing so much as to crawl off into some obscure hole to nurse his homesickness, was forced to muster a smile and to bow his stiff little bow.

Rubinstein's blue eyes, with their oddly dreamy expression (which gossip said came from working all day and staying up to play cards at the English Club all night), missed no detail of his young assistant's frayed cuffs and threadbare linen shirt when Tchaikovsky took off the heavy coat and made ready to meet his fellow teachers in Rubinstein's apartment. The corners of the ironical Rubinstein mouth twitched as he noted the diffident, shy way in which Tchaikovsky greeted the men of music assembled to look him over.

"Probably has more talent for composing than any other man here, and yet he is frightened out of his wits at being surrounded by so many famous faces." Rubinstein, who had assembled these famous faces, whose job it was to keep the Conservatory going so that these talents should be able to draw the modest fees which kept them from starvation, smiled his half-mocking, half-sympathetic smile as he made introductions.

First of all there was Constantine Albrecht, who held the post of Inspector of the Conservatory. He was a cellist, who had played with the orchestra at the Opera House since he was fifteen years old, a talented musician and good teacher, Rubinstein's right-hand at the Conservatory.

Albrecht clasped Tchaikovsky's hand and spoke hearty words of greeting. These two warmed to each other immediately. This meeting at Rubinstein's was the beginning of a lifelong friendship.

Music publisher P. I. Jurgenson, Nicholas Rubinstein's stanch friend and supporter of the Conservatory, was present too. He was the first Russian publisher to bring out the works of the classical school of Western Europe in cheap editions so that music could be bought by others than the aristocracy and wealthy merchant class. With few exceptions, Tchaikovsky's published compositions were all brought out by Jurgenson's firm.

Nicholas Kashkin, young Professor of Pianoforte, greeted Tchaikovsky with the cordiality of an old comrade; for Laroche, the friend of both, had painted a good and accurate portrait of the newcomer. Hubert, old friend of St. Petersburg schooldays, was a welcome familiar presence in the roomful of strangers. Osberg, the teacher of singing, was cordial and friendly.

Kindly old Alexander, Rubinstein's servant, smiled his own special welcome for the shy young man and apologized when his white cat entered the room and jumped unceremoniously into Tchaikovsky's lap.

"Never mind!" Tchaikovsky motioned the old man away with a smile. "Let *koshka* stay."

Such little things can make a stranger feel at home. For Tchaikovsky his real welcome to Moscow lay in an old man's smile and the purring of a white cat.

For the first few days Tchaikovsky stayed at the Hotel Kokorev, but Rubinstein soon arranged matters more to his own liking. For all his air of independence and competence, Rubinstein dreaded living alone. Most of his friends were either married and established in households of their own or, being aware of Rubinstein's odd habits of entertaining almost without cessation and staying up to all hours, had tactfully but firmly refused his invitations to share his apartment. Tchaikovsky was unprepared with arguments, even had he felt their need, and gladly accepted the Director's importunate invitation.

Established in a little bedroom divided from Rubinstein's room by a thin partition, Tchaikovsky wrote his twin brothers: "Truth to tell, I am afraid the scratching of my pen must disturb him. I sit at home all day, and Rubinstein, who leads rather an excitable life, cannot sufficiently marvel at my industry. . . . Sometimes I feel rather melancholy, but as a rule I am possessed by an insatiable craving for work, which is my greatest consolation."

The work which Tchaikovsky's pen scratched away at was the Overture in C minor, which he had sketched out during the summer. He was eager to finish the orchestration for two reasons: Rubinstein had promised that if the music were good enough he would have it performed by the Musical Society of Moscow. More important, however, was the fact that his classes would begin after the preliminary examinations of the students on January 14, and then teaching, not composing, would be his main task for a while.

Tchaikovsky's reach exceeded his grasp, in this instance. Rubinstein did not think the Overture good enough to merit performance and frankly told his young professor so. Tchaikovsky sent the manuscript off to Laroche in St. Petersburg, with the request that Anton Rubinstein be persuaded to give the music a place at one of his concerts. Laroche reported that Anton greeted the suggestion with his usual mocking bow, and refused to play his former pupil's music. The conductor of the opera concerts in St. Petersburg also refused to give the music a place on his program. It was not, therefore, with a triumphant feeling of success that Tchaikovsky took up his duties at the Conservatory.

His first morning at the Conservatory was a distressing ordeal. Most of the young students who presented themselves for the entrance examinations were pretty young girls, daughters of the wealthy families of Moscow. They were very confident of themselves, and giggled behind their hands at the awkward, shy, out-at-elbows new teacher. Tchaikovsky, who had had very few friends among girls and women, and who furthermore shared the sad misconception of nineteenth-century masculinity that women were strange creatures, likely in all matters to be trivial and insincere, and in artistic matters to be hopelessly inadequate, looked at these girls as upon creatures from the moon, did not know what to say to them, ended by feeling that he disliked them heartily.

Rubinstein, who understood well the value of giving the appearance of success in a world which accorded respect only to those who could make money, insisted that Tchaikovsky get some new clothes. Writing to his brothers concerning a party he attended, Peter Ilich said:

". . . I did not take part in the dancing, although I was attired in Rubinstein's dress-coat. The latter looks after me like a nurse, and insists upon doing so. Today he forced me to accept half a dozen shirts (you need not mention this to the Davydovs or anyone else), and tomorrow he will carry me off to his tailor to order me a frock-coat."

Gradually Tchaikovsky's nervousness in the classroom subsided. He grew accustomed to the girl students, though he persisted in his scornful attitude toward them. For their part the girls soon tired of their jokes at the new teacher's expense. They looked on him with admiration at times, for in his new clothes he cut a handsome figure; besides, he was not one to accept slapdash work, and the least earnest of the students dropped out, leaving the more careful, serious students in his classes.

Despite his rather superior attitude toward his pupils, Tchaikovsky never for a moment relaxed his efforts to be a good teacher. He was never satisfied with himself in this respect, and often complained to the friends at home that he was not fitted for his profession. The fact is, he tried too hard. He wished to make a composer of every student, and all that most of them wanted was to learn to be adequate teachers themselves. He insisted upon prodigious amounts of work, and flew into a rage if he detected a lapse of interest in the lectures, or the tendency in a student to do work inferior to his talents or knowledge.

The students shrugged their shoulders at his rages, frowned

at the long exercises in harmony, smiled sometimes at the earnestness of his lectures, but nevertheless respected him. And the reason was one that Rubinstein if not Tchaikovsky knew full well: Tchaikovsky was an excellent teacher, with a wealth of information and illustrative material at his finger tips. He was always crystal-clear in his explanations, making his points with the precision of an accountant adding figures. But even more than his precision, the way he lost himself to the world when he argued a point dear to him before his class was a joy to his students. Years later he wrote a letter to a friend in the delightful manner he used in his classroom.

"You ask me about melodies built upon the notes of the harmony," he said. "I can assure you, and prove it by many examples, that it is quite possible, by means of rhythm and the transposition of these notes, to evolve millions of new and beautiful melodic combinations." Thus he stated the conclusion which he was now prepared to prove by the evidence of illustration.

"In the music of Beethoven, Weber, Mendelssohn, Schumann, and especially Wagner, we frequently find melodies which consist of the notes of the common chord; a gifted musician will always be able to invent a new and interesting fanfare. Do you remember the beautiful Sword-motive in the *Nibelungen?*

"I am very fond of a melody by Verdi (a very gifted man) :

"How glorious and how fresh the chief theme of the first movement of Rubinstein's *Ocean* Symphony:

"If I racked my brains a little, I should find countless examples to support my assertion. Talent is the sole secret. It knows no limitations: it creates the most beautiful music out of nothing. Could there be anything more trivial than the following melody?

"Or Glinka, the *Jota aragonesa:*

"And yet what splendid musical structures Beethoven and Glinka have raised on these themes!"

With the confidence that good clothes gave him and the knowledge that his students admired him and his colleagues in the Conservatory respected him, Tchaikovsky became quite cheerful. From this time on he began to display a trait that eventually became as much a part of him as the stiff little bow and the kindly smile which did not light up the sad eyes: when he was happy and contented he always set to work at composing like a very demon. His pen continued to "scratch" during these early Conservatory days, and the work that took form on the music sheets was his first Symphony in G major, which he called *Winter Daydreams* (Opus 13).

Nicholas Rubinstein sometimes rebelled at Tchaikovsky's persistent application to his work. At such times there was no going against the wishes of the willful Director of the Conservatory. Almost by main force he would carry Peter Ilich off with him to some gay restaurant—the Praga, the Hermitage, or the Yar. These places were like clubs, or the old coffeehouses of eighteenth-century England. Friends met to eat and drink and to talk politics and art. And while they talked, gypsy orchestras played and sang. Hot, steamy air, incessant murmuring of earnest voices, laughter, a toast drunk to this and that, and the music of the gypsies—music which begins on a slow, melancholy note and grows gradually faster until it is wild, abandoned, almost frenzied—such was the Bohemian life which Tchaikovsky and Rubinstein enjoyed in the evenings after work.

For your frol - ic and your games I have no heart;

14

There could have been no more merciless taskmaster than Tchaikovsky was, where his work was concerned. The symphony, begun with such feeling of elation, began to give him trouble, but difficulties did not slow the scratching pen. Far into the night he worked, dousing his head in cold water with the dawn, going to his classes at the Conservatory without a wink of sleep to rest him. Rubinstein shook his head, but something in Tchaikovsky's feverish manner kept him silent.

The composer's friends, fearing that he was ruining his health with the long hours of work, no sleep, and constant thinking on his troublesome creative problem, tried to persuade him to attend parties, informal musical evenings. Out of deference to Nicholas Rubinstein and the close friends like Kashkin and his wife, Tchaikovsky went to some of the social functions which kept Moscow up every night until dawn, but he was seldom good company, preferring to seek some quiet corner where he could go back to thinking about his symphony. He dreaded the enormous dinners which he was ex-

pected to share with such lusty eaters as Rubinstein. A letter
to Anatol voiced his protests:

"Try as I may, it is impossible to lead a quiet life in Moscow, where one must overeat and drink. This is the fifth day
in succession that I have come home late with an overloaded
stomach." And he hastened to add: "But you must not
imagine that I am idle: from breakfast till the midday meal
I work without a break."

When the spring vacation came, at the end of March,
Tchaikovsky needed rest desperately. He hurried off to St.
Petersburg to spend the Easter holidays with his father. He
was little rested by the trip, however; a certain uneasiness prevailed where groups of friends met together in drawing-rooms
or acquaintances stopped to chat in clusters at the street
corners. The great Russian Bear was stirring, and presently
all this unrest found violent expression. Karakovich, a Pole,
attempted to kill the Tsar.

Tchaikovsky heard the news on his way back to Moscow.
His reaction was one of indignation. He shared Nicholas
Davydov's view that the Tsar and his advisers were not re-
sponsible for the ills of the people, that if these ills could be
called to the Tsar's attention, everything would be straight-
ened out.

His dismay was shared, though for a different reason, by
Russians who would have liked to see Tsardom abolished and
a democracy established. The wise ones kept saying that
killing a Tsar was not the way to change the system of which
he was figurehead.

For the summer vacation in 1876, Tchaikovsky had intended to visit his sister at Kamenka, but a late thaw and early
rains had made muddy rivers of the roads. The public coaches
suspended their schedules, so that it would have been necessary for the composer to hire a private carriage for a large

part of the trip. His fifty-ruble salary was not equal to the strain. Instead, money was found to send Anatol to his sister's, and Peter Ilich joined Modeste and Father Ilya in a visit to the generous Davydov family—Mother Alexandra, Elizabeth, and Vera—at Miatlev in the Lake Ladoga region.

Tchaikovsky's frayed nerves were soothed as he walked in the evergreen forests of the Finnish shore, and explored the marshes from which ducks and geese and smaller marsh birds rose in clouds whenever a boat nosed its way among the reeds and willows. He enjoyed the blue-gray of the northern sky, the wine-sharpness of the wind on the water, the sparkling clarity of the sunshine; yet he was not at peace with himself. Fanny Dürbach would have recognized the trouble. She would have remembered the little boy who had tossed feverishly in his bed and moaned, "Oh, this music. It gives me no peace!"

By the end of June Tchaikovsky had a nervous breakdown. The doctors were grave, warned the composer that he must give up working at night, confided to his family that he had narrowly escaped madness. Good nursing worked its miracle, and the composer was able to return to his classes; but the cure was not complete. From this time on the slightest illness could produce strange hallucinations amounting to delirium. His letters are full of references to these seizures during his travels, when he alarmed fellow passengers on trains and often had to leave his coach at some little town on the way.

On his way back to school from Miatlev, Tchaikovsky called on Anton Rubinstein, hoping to get a word of praise for *Winter Daydreams*. Anton looked at the nearly completed symphony and bluntly called it poor stuff. Concealing his bitter disappointment as best he could, Peter Ilich rolled up his manuscript and went on his way.

Anton Rubinstein's persistent hostility as an artist had

finally put steel into Tchaikovsky, who believed in himself.
There was no slightest trace of personal animosity or resentment in this new attitude of Tchaikovsky's. Anton never
ceased to be in his estimation a great teacher, a great artist,
and a great though sadly aloof man. The younger composer
merely had come to accept the fact that his music did not
strike a sympathetic chord in Anton, that just as he himself
could not understand why Brahms was regarded as a genius,
the great Anton could not value the work of his celebrated
pupil at its true worth.

Nicholas Rubinstein had been playing politics as usual,
and a new building for the Conservatory was being constructed by wealthy patrons. Opening of the school and
auditorium was marked by a banquet attended by the leaders
of Moscow society. At Tchaikovsky's insistence, the first
music heard in the new hall was Glinka's overture to *Russlan
and Ludmilla*, played impromptu by the young professor of
harmony.

In its larger quarters the Conservatory grew by leaps and
bounds. New teachers were being added to the faculty: Laub,
Wieniawski, Kossman, Dubuque, Anton Door. Rubinstein
was working like a dynamo. The new professors were often at
his house, studying his proposals, his suggestions, his outlines
for their work in the Conservatory. Wealthy patrons like
Prince Odoevsky, who became one of Tchaikovsky's close
friends, came often to discuss financial matters. Visiting musicians intruded at all hours. Most of these people took it for
granted that they were welcome at any time to talk to Tchaikovsky also in his little room. Therefore, when Rubinstein
suggested that Peter Ilich undertake the writing of an overture to celebrate the coming betrothal of the Tsarevitch and
the Princess Dagmar of Denmark, the composer had to leave
his little monk's cell in Rubinstein's apartment and take him-

self off to a neighboring inn, "The Great Britain," which had few patrons during the daytime. There in some quiet corner he would order tea, set down his inkwell, and unroll his music paper.

Tchaikovsky was well pleased with this overture, Opus 15, which he had built around the Danish National Hymn. The old desire to get a nod of approval from Anton Rubinstein overcame his better judgment. He sent the manuscript to St. Petersburg. Anton coldly turned down the proposal that the piece be given a place at one of the Musical Society concerts.

The Danish Overture was actually performed in February 1867 in St. Petersburg. The critics of that city tore it to pieces. The malice of their remarks stunned Tchaikovsky. He had a long memory for injury if it concerned his art; never afterward did he expect or solicit recognition in the city of the Baltic. When many years later his works were enthusiastically received there, it was too late to heal the wound.

When, after five student years of denying himself every luxury, the composer's sincerest efforts were rewarded by cold indifference to his work in St. Petersburg, and by overwork and direst poverty in Moscow, his spirit faltered. He complained to Anatol: "All last week I was out of humor; first, because of the bad weather; secondly, from shortness of money. . . ."

In the summer of 1867 Peter Ilich determined to have a holiday. With about fifty dollars in his pocket, he set off hopefully with Anatol to spend the summer in Finland. At the end of a few days in a hotel in Viborg they were nearly penniless.

There followed a series of semicomic adventures. Spending their last few rubles, the brothers went back to St. Petersburg. What was their horror to discover that their father, whom they had expected to come to the rescue, was spending his

vacation in the Ural Mountains. Peter and Anatol had only
a few small coins left and nowhere to go in St. Petersburg,
since most of their friends and relatives had gone to country
homes for the summer.

"What shall we do now?" Anatol looked with frightened
eyes at his elder brother.

Peter Ilich, very near to panic himself, suddenly thought
of Vera Davydov.

"How much money have we between us?" he asked.

They counted their resources. There were just enough
kopeks to buy a "between-decks" passage on a Lake Ladoga
steamer to Hapsal, where Vera and her mother were living.

The wind was sharp on the water, and neither brother was
dressed warmly enough. Peter Ilich managed to persuade a
fellow passenger to lend Anatol a blanket. He himself walked
up and down, up and down, all night, shivering, hungry, rail-
ing at fate and his lack of foresight.

The Davydovs proved themselves real friends. They welcomed the tired travelers and insisted that both spend the
entire summer at Hapsal. Once the uncomfortable experiences were in the past, Peter Ilich could see the ironic
humor of them, and made Vera laugh until the tears came
when he related the mishaps. He himself was abjectly grateful, however, for Vera's life-saving invitation and settled
down with a sigh of relief into the peaceful home.

In the evening he and Vera played duets or read aloud
from the works of Alfred de Musset. Mornings they sometimes accompanied Anatol on fishing expeditions. The beauty
of the lake country and the tactful kindness of his friends re-
stored Tchaikovsky's confidence. Happiness meant a return
to work.

He composed a work for the piano—two melodies which
he called "The Ruined Chateau" and "Song Without

Words." These, together with a "Scherzo" dating back to the student days, he published later as Opus 2, calling the work *Souvenir of Hapsal* and dedicating it to Vera Davydov.

The "Song Without Words," No. 3 of the opus, is one of the world's favorite melodies, a fitting tribute to a friendship which needed no words for understanding:

When the summer stipend arrived from the Conservatory in Moscow, Tchaikovsky said good-by to Hapsal. With Anatol established in his school again the composer prepared to take up his teaching duties once more.

The contrast of the Moscow life with the idyllic existence at Hapsal was painful. Tchaikovsky wanted desperately to get away from Nicholas Rubinstein's home, where confusion and excitement reigned twenty-four hours a day; but the Director would not hear of a change, pointing out that Peter Ilich did not make enough money to support a separate establishment anyway. The composer concealed his irritation as best he could, though he was sorely bothered by the fact that he found little time for writing music.

Rubinstein carried him off nearly every evening to receptions or Bohemian gatherings in stuffy restaurants and clubs. Life in Moscow seemed to be going on quite indifferent to the important events affecting Russia's destiny that year. Who cared that the Tsar had sold Alaska to the United States for $7,200,000? What did it matter that Canada had become

a dominion, that in England the city workers had at last received the right to vote? And that eccentric German econ-
omist, Karl Marx—what was this about his having completed
one volume of his work *Capital? Nichevo!*

About this time Tchaikovsky met the great Russian dramatist Ostrovsky, amused him by telling about the student
composition inspired by *The Storm* which had brought
thunder and lightning out of Anton the Great. It was Ostrovsky who provided the libretto for the composer's first
opera *The Voivode.*

There was a famine in Siberia in 1867. Thousands of
peasants were starving. While the government bureaus were
holding discussions as to possible relief measures, private organizations tried to do something. The musicians of Moscow
agreed to donate their talents to a charity concert. Tchaikovsky, for all his timidity, agreed to conduct the "Dances" from
The Voivode. Kashkin reported the outcome of the composer's public debut:

". . . I noticed that he was quite distracted; he came on
timidly, as though he would have been glad to hide, or run
away, and, on mounting to the conductor's desk, looked like
a man who finds himself in some desperate situation. Apparently his composition was blotted out from his mind; he
did not see the score before him, and gave all the leads at the
wrong moment, or to the wrong instruments. Fortunately,
the band knew the music so well that they paid no attention
whatever to Tchaikovsky's beat but, laughing in their sleeves,
got through the dances very creditably in spite of him." Ten
years elapsed before Tchaikovsky took up the baton in public
again.

At this same concert where terror-stricken Peter Ilich made
his ignoble debut, Rimsky-Korsakov's *Serbian Fantasia* was
played. Next day the prominent music publication in Mos-

cow, *Entr'acte*, came out with a blistering criticism of the Rimsky-Korsakov work. Tchaikovsky's work was praised as the work of a "mature musician."

A mean, petty nature might have rejoiced at this trouncing given to a member of "The Five," who had taken every opportunity to call Tchaikovsky's work commonplace. Not so Tchaikovsky, who was always able to forget himself where truth in art was concerned.

What is more, the personal equation had entered the picture. At rehearsals for the charity concert Tchaikovsky met both Rimsky-Korsakov and Balakirev, leader of the New School, and surprised himself by liking his "enemies" immensely. In Rimsky-Korsakov he recognized a highly gifted composer and a warmly sympathetic nature.

Before Peter Ilich had recovered from his own public "disgrace," he sat down to his desk and wrote an answer to the unfavorable criticism of his fellow composer. Published in *Entr'acte*, this answer aroused much favorable comment.

At Easter time in 1867, when Tchaikovsky visited his father, he was surprised to receive the friendliest overtures from "The Five," who invited him to attend their sessions at the home of their sponsor Dargomijsky. From that time on, Tchaikovsky met the members of the new Russian school on friendly terms, often praised their works in his writings, and frequently invited their suggestions concerning his own work, but never once gave up his own views to embrace theirs.

The article contributed to *Entr'acte* had an unforeseen result. The editors asked Tchaikovsky to undertake a weekly series of musical criticisms. The opportunity to guide the musical thought of Russia could not be refused by a sincere artist, even though the pay was small and the work none too easy. Without complaint, Tchaikovsky added this new task to his already heavy burden of work.

Ru - bles ten times ten: that shall be your fee.

15

A brief interlude in the form of a trip abroad, and Tchaikovsky was back with his nose to the grindstone in Moscow. During the next year he worked, as he himself expressed it in a letter to Modeste, "like a slave." His salary rose to 1400 rubles. Though he could not summon the courage to move from Rubinstein's, his increased income gave him more independence in everyday affairs.

Back and forth, back and forth—from bare little room where *Fatum* (Destiny), a symphonic poem published in later years as Opus 77, was being set down with painstaking care, to the classrooms at the Conservatory, where the mysteries of counterpoint and harmony were being explained with no less care—Tchaikovsky's neat boots took him day after day between September and January. Before they had time to wear too deep a rut on the road between work and work, however, two important happenings occurred which cast Tchaikovsky's well-ordered life into temporary chaos.

The first event was an announcement by the directors of

the Moscow Opera of a proposed performance of *The Voivode*. The composer was called from his classroom to the theater one day to discover that two choral rehearsals had already been given and the first solo rehearsal was about to take place.

The second event was the coming of an Italian opera company for an indefinite engagement in Moscow. There was nothing remarkable about this company, but there was something decidedly remarkable about one of the singers—Désirée Artôt. She had a beautiful voice, described as being in timbre more like the oboe than the flute. She was not pretty, but she possessed fine dramatic talent, and about her acting as about her singing there was something indescribably warm and sensitive.

Tchaikvosky betrayed his state of mind where this singer was concerned in a letter to Anatol. He began by telling Anatol the plot of an opera which Ostrovsky proposed to write for him:

"The scene is laid in Babylon and Greece, in the time of Alexander of Macedon, who is introduced as one of the characters. We have representatives of two great races of antiquity: the Hebrews and the Greeks. . . . You have no idea what a fine plot it is! Just now I am writing a symphonic sketch, *Fatum*. The Italian opera is creating a furore. Artôt is a splendid creature. She and I are good friends."

When Babylon and Greece, the Hebrews and Alexander of Macedon, become mixed with symphonic sketches and Italian operas and "splendid creatures" like Artôt—the answer, said practical Anatol to himself, is that brother Peter Ilich is in love.

The news spread fast among members of the family. Sasha was anxious. Father Ilya was delighted. The twins were curious. Laroche and the other Moscow friends were inclined to tease. In short, no one was surprised when Peter Ilich and Désirée became engaged.

No one was surprised, but two were not pleased—Désirée's mother and Nicholas Rubinstein.

"This is nonsense!" Désirée's mother exploded. "You are already famous; this composer of yours is a nobody. You make money; he is penniless. What can you be thinking of? He will expect you to give up your career, live all your life here, in Russia!"

As for Nicholas Rubinstein, he was in a towering rage. "Peter Ilich! You must be mad! This woman—this singer—she will never consent to give up her career. And what does this career of hers mean? It means constant traveling all over Europe. It means that if you are together, you must follow her around like a French poodle. It means that you will be a shadow of Désirée Artôt!"

When Peter Ilich talked all this over with his beloved, she looked as sad as he, shook her head at his timid proposal that she consider giving up the stage.

"It is my life, Petia. I should be lost without it. And Mama is right in one respect. I have grown used to making a good living. I like to spend money. I should be bitterly unhappy without it. But I know we can work this problem out. Petia, let us wait until summer. I shall go on with my tour, you with your work. Then we shall meet at my country home near Paris and decide the whole affair."

Poor Father Ilya was distressed to hear this news. He wrote a letter full of kindly, common-sense advice. He ended by urging his son to marry Désirée if he loved her and let no nonsense about being her shadow stand in his way.

Peter Ilich for his part was desperately unhappy. The one great weakness in his character was betraying him: He was unable to make up his own mind or to take a firm stand

Je sens mon cœur qui bat, qui bat,
Je ne sais pas pourquoi!
Pique Dame, Act II, Scene 4.

against the opinions of others in matters affecting his private life. Opinions blew upon him like prankish winds upon this-tledown, and he moved now this way, now that, according to which breeze was the stronger.

This tempest which raged over his and Désirée's head had a most unfortunate effect on the fortunes of *The Voivode*. The composer was too upset to bother with directing the work, particularly when the chorus of the opera was doing double duty, with the Moscow Opera and with the Italian company, and so could not give him more than half an ear at rehearsals. He called the performance off. His method was simplicity itself: He merely refused to deliver the complete score.

Désirée went away. Peter walked around like a man in a dream. He composed one piece, the hauntingly beautiful *Romance* in F minor, Opus 5. This plaintive melody for piano he dedicated to Désirée.

The meeting in Paris never took place. Désirée Artôt, im-patient perhaps at so undecided a suitor, was married to the baritone singer Padilla at Warsaw, without a word of explana-tion to Peter Ilich. The news was a severe shock to Tchai-kovsky. A year later, when Désirée returned to sing in Mos-cow, the composer attended a performance with his friend Kashkin.

"When, in 1869, Artôt reappeared at the Moscow Opera,"

Kashkin reported on the event, "I sat in the stalls next to Tchaikovsky, who was greatly moved. When the singer came on, he held his opera glasses to his eyes and never lowered them during the entire performance; but he must have seen very little, for tear after tear rolled down his cheeks."

Tchaikovsky threw himself feverishly into work to forget Désirée. In February 1869, *The Voivode* was at last given in Moscow. It was a tremendous success with first-night audiences and the composer was recalled fifteen times. The success was a flash in the pan, however; the critics set to work to demolish it. Ultimately the composer destroyed the work. Only fragments have survived as Opus 3 and Opus 78.

Laroche, who had become a music critic in Moscow after the schooldays in St. Petersburg, had the poor taste to choose this particular time to sneer at his friend's art. The composer was shocked to read that it was not only the opera but Tchaikovsky's talent in general which was disparaged. The review caused a rift between the two which never really closed. There was one friend less in Russia for Tchaikovsky after that.

Fatum was completed, dedicated to Balakirev, who had succeeded Anton Rubinstein as director of the Musical Society, and duly performed by that society. Critic Cui and the rest of "The Five" condemned the work, though Balakirev wrote to assure the composer that he was flattered by the dedication.

Tchaikovsky smiled wryly. In musical controversy, he reflected, he was between the devil and the deep sea. Laroche condemned *Fatum* because it was not in the classic mold. "The Five" laid its weaknesses to the composer's lack of "modernism." Tchaikovsky eventually decided that *Fatum* was "rubbish" and destroyed the score.

Other works took form under his feverish hands. *Waltz Caprice*, Opus 4, for piano. *Undine*, an opera begun in January 1869 and completed by the end of July at Kamenka. This opera failed to please the composer, and it met the fate of *The Voivode* and *Fatum*. Parts of it he preserved, however. Fragments of *Undine* were used in the incidental music to a fairy ballet called *The Snow Maiden*, Opus 12. The wedding march became a part of the Second Symphony, Opus 17. The love duet became the *adagio* of the *Swan Lake Ballet*, Opus 20.

The restless pen scratched on. Twenty-five Russian folk-songs were arranged for piano duet at publisher Jurgenson's request. By March 1870, the romantic overture-fantasy *Romeo and Juliet*, based on the Shakespeare play, was completed.

There is little doubt that the image of Désirée Artôt was a very real presence in the little room where Tchaikovsky wrote the music which describes a tragic youthful love. In this orchestral fantasy, Tchaikovsky for the first time displayed his individuality. Here he began to hit his stride. In subjective music, descriptive of the emotions of the human soul, Tchaikovsky always achieved his happiest effects. Such is the music of *Romeo and Juliet*.

The overture opens with a quiet mood tinged with melancholy, the subdued tones of clarinets and bassoons calling up the figure of kindly, sympathetic Friar Laurence. There follows a passage of ominous foreboding. Then the music quickens, becomes boisterous and contentious to portray the conflict of the opposing houses of Capulet and Montague. The tumult subsides, and a songlike melody emerges. The English horn and muted violas voice Romeo's yearning cry: "O starry night of ecstasy!" The music depicting strife and violence returns, reaching a climax of tumultuous fury. Then Romeo's song rises above the strife, anguished and lamenting. The overture ends in an ominous roll of drums and crashing chords to suggest the tragic end of the story of star-crossed lovers.

Tchaikovsky was badly in need of a rest and a change of scene when the invitation came to join his friend and favorite pupil, Vladimir Shilovsky, in Paris. Shilovsky, ill with tuberculosis, was taking mineral baths at Soden. They had time to take a few of these curative baths, attend a Beethoven festival in Mannheim, city of Mozart memories, and visit Nicholas Rubinstein on vacation in Wiesbaden before the Franco-Prussian War broke out. With hundreds of others, Peter Ilich and Shilovsky fled to neutral Switzerland, just as people have been fleeing in wartime to this little mountain country ever since.

This war, which ended in the downfall of Louis Napoleon —the Emperor Napoleon III—and his dreams of empire in Mexico and other sections of the globe, raged for a year. Before it ended, the workers of Paris had set up a socialist state which they called the Commune, swept away almost immediately by those who preferred the parliamentary forms of the Third French Republic. At the end of the war, Germany was a united state with one emperor rather than the loose federation it had been.

While all this history was in process of being made, Tchaikovsky and his companion stayed for six weeks in the quiet village of Interlaken, which, as its name indicates ("between lakes"), lies between Lake Thun and Lake Brienz, in the valley of the Aar. The Aar is a rushing, sparkling mountain stream, an unruly little river with a dash of impudence. Interlaken, one of the favorite resorts of Canton Bern, is built around an ancient monastery of the Augustine Friars, dating from the year 1130. The hamlet sets its frame houses with their carved wooden balconies and overhanging stories at rakish angles on the Alpine meadows. In the distance, to the south, the white peak of the Jungfrau rises to meet the blue sky.

"Nu, Volodya!" laughed Peter Ilich. "For the first time in years I feel like singing. Here we are, two Russian bears, in the Canton of the Bear. Plenty of Swiss cheese for you—you who are without a soul. Plenty of mountains, glaciers, blue skies, downy white edelweiss growing next to snow banks for me!"

The sorrow which Peter Ilich had smothered in the music of *Romeo and Juliet* was buried and forgotten in the pleasant village life of Interlaken. Mornings found the composer dressed in stout breeches and leather coat, with Alpine stock and rucksack, and Tirolese feather in his cap, wandering blissfully across meadows fragrant with wild Alpine grasses. Sometimes he walked along the Aar, contrasting its sparkling clearness with the muddy sluggishness of the Tiasmin River at Kamenka, smiling as he reflected that for all its ugliness the river which flowed past the beloved haven where his sister lived was dearer to him than any other.

Evenings found him in the little garden of the inn, sipping wine and listening with naive delight to the clanging of zither strings under sturdy peasant fingers, and the hearty rhythms of accordions. Nearly every evening the peasant lads and lasses from the village dressed up in costume and danced the traditional Swiss dances for the visitors at the inn—*Schuhplattlers*, *Ländlers*, wedding dances, and Swiss "valsers." When the hour grew late, the broom dance swept both performers and visitors out of the lower rooms of the inn to make way for the mop-and-pail brigade.

Tchaikovsky returned to Russia by way of Munich, where he stopped off to visit his old friend Prince Galitsin, and Vienna, where the railroad routes from St. Petersburg, Berlin, Paris, and Rome met and crossed. The gay city on the Danube had just the air of unhurried industry which pleased

Tchaikovsky best, and the carefree, hearty way which is known in German as *Gemütlichkeit.* The composer was almost sorry to leave Vienna, though already the urge to get to work stirred him strangely.

No sooner were the bags and trunks unpacked in Russia than the busy pen began to move once more. Before the year of 1870 was over five important works were completed: *Six Songs,* Opus 6; *Valse Scherzo* for piano, Opus 7; *Capriccio* in G flat for piano, Opus 8; *Three Pieces for Piano,* Opus 9; and the song "So Soon Forgotten." And besides, he began work on a new opera *The Oprichnik.*

Perhaps none of these works is more eloquent than No. 6 of *Six Songs.* This is the well-known "None but the Lonely Heart."

Early in 1871, Tchaikovsky found himself, as usual, painfully short of money. Nicholas Rubinstein suggested that he organize a concert. Since none of his works was suitable for small orchestra or ensemble and he could not afford to hire a whole symphony orchestra, Tchaikovsky sat down to compose a work for instrumental quartet. The result was the First String Quartet, in D major, Opus 11.

When the work was given in March, with Laub leading the Musical Society's quartet and good friend Nicholas Rubinstein at the piano, a very great man was in the audience. This was I. S. Turgeniev, author of the idol-smashing novel of the '60's *Fathers and Children.*

Heads popped up all over the house on necks stretched to

see the Russian huntsman who brought such a keen eye, such a sharp ear, such a quick hand on the trigger to the literary scene, who startled aristocratic circles by his description of the age in which he lived:

"The new was taking root with difficulty; the old had lost all power; the dishonest jostled the incompetent; life, shaken to its foundations, rocked like a quagmire, and only one great word 'freedom' moved like the spirit of God upon the face of the waters."

Turgeniev must have found much that was new and honest and free and hopeful in Tchaikovsky's music, for he praised it highly.

The composition that received the great writer's attention and the public's unanimous approval had a story behind it. In 1869, when Tchaikovsky attended his brother Hippolite's wedding at Kamenka, he heard a carpenter on the estate singing the folk-song *Vanya*. Its words went like this:

> "Late at night sat Ivan
> Sadly on the divan,
> In his hand he held a glass of rum;
> There he drowned his sorrow,
> There forgot the morrow,
> Dreamed of love and happiness to come."

The lightly careless words were sung to a tune so plaintive and "Russian" that the composer jotted it down. The entire melody is used in the *Andante Cantabile* of the First String Quartet.

That summer Tchaikovsky set out like a happy schoolboy to visit brother Nicholas at Konotop, and Anatol and Modeste at Kiev. He and Modeste traveled together to see Sasha in Kamenka. From there Peter Ilich went to Nizy to visit his friend Kondratiev, and wound up the summer in Ussovo, where fragile Shilovsky welcomed him with pathetic eagerness.

At Nizy, Tchaikovsky finished his remarkable textbook on harmony, which was immediately adopted by both Russian conservatories. At Ussovo, where he could walk under the trees at sundown and through the dews in the pastures at sunup, he rested and gathered his forces for another year of living in a restless world.

There he drown'd his sor - row,   There for - got   the mor - row,

16

The year 1872 was an important milestone in Tchaikovsky's life. That was the year he achieved independence. Money, which makes the mare go for artists as well as for other workers, was the basis of the thirty-two-year-old composer's new freedom.

His earnings at the Conservatory had risen well above 1500 rubles a year. From the Russian Musical Society, which at Nicholas Rubinstein's insistence paid 200 to 300 rubles for each new work performed at their symphony concerts, and from the sale of the music editions published by Jurgenson, he received 500 rubles more. Added to this income was the payment from the magazines for his work as music critic. All in all, he made more than 2000 rubles a year—about $1000— a tremendous increase over the 600 rubles ($300) a year which had been his total income when he first came to the Conservatory in Moscow.

When he realized that at last he had enough money to afford rooms of his own, the composer's first thought was to find someone to take his place at Rubinstein's. Though Tchaikovsky admired his friend's artistry and executive ability and was grateful for his kindnesses, he had suffered in numerous small ways at this despot's hands. Peter Ilich longed to get out from under the yoke imposed by a will stronger than his own. N. A. Hubert came forward as substitute. Trying as hard as he could to hide his elation at the thought of being free, Tchaikovsky went looking for rooms.

When he found suitable rooms, he began to look for furnishings. Everything was selected more with comfort than beauty in mind, and the result was anything but sumptuous. A large sofa, a few cheap chairs, a table, and a small bed— this was his furniture. For decorations he hung two pictures: The Dauphin in the house of the shoemaker Simon, given the composer by Begichev in Paris; and a portrait of Anton Rubinstein, given him by the painter Madame Bonné.

Tchaikovsky was delighted with the result. Only one thing more remained to be attended to: A servant must be engaged. The composer was determined to begin his new life in proper style.

Michael Sofronov, a peasant from the village of Maidanovo near Moscow, a kindly, capable, dependable man, accepted the small wage which Tchaikovsky was able to pay. This man remained with the composer for many years. He came as a servant, stayed on as a friend. Tchaikovsky never lost sight of him, even after Michael left his employ and was replaced by his brother Alexis. Both men played an important part in the composer's life, treating him like a younger brother, never questioning his wishes, looking after his interests, never listening to his music. Tchaikovsky, like the Norwegian Edvard Grieg, could not bear critics in the household.

With money in his pocket and quiet surroundings for his work, Tchaikovsky began to gain real confidence in himself.

He walked with a lighter step to the Conservatory, flew into rages with his pupils less frequently, cut his beard more stylishly, and wrote fewer letters complaining (as he had been doing for years) that he was bored with teaching, that life in Moscow was too exciting, that he longed for nothing so much as to retire to a farm, that he was getting old.

Just as the newness was wearing off the experience of living his own life in his own way, Vladimir Shilovsky appeared with the proposal that Tchaikovsky get leave-of-absence from the Conservatory and spend a month with him in Nice. Rubinstein, who understood the value of keeping the friendship of such wealthy patrons of the Conservatory as this former student, granted the leave.

Without knowing quite how it happened, the composer found himself settled in luxurious quarters in the gay French resort on the Mediterranean Sea. He wrote letters home, telling how odd it seemed to come from the depths of a Russian winter to a land where orange trees bloomed. He complained a little of the too-gay life he led with his companion, but the next instant he was praising the beauties of the warm mornings when he strolled along the seashore or wandered along the narrow, winding streets of the old town, which lies on the left bank of the small Paillon River.

It would not have been like Tchaikovsky to idle. While he was in Nice, he composed two charming pieces for piano, which he dedicated to his friend Shilovsky. These were *Nocturne* and *Humoresque*, published as Opus 10.

By March he was back in Moscow, working hard at *The Oprichnik*, the opera based on the life of Ivan the Terrible. In May the score was sent off to the directors of the St. Petersburg opera. The composer had to possess his soul in patience for two years before he learned how the public would like his opera. The work was not presented until 1874. Its success then was brilliant. The entire faculties of both the Moscow and the St. Petersburg conservatories attended in a body. These honors did not please the composer half so much as the fact that his old father was present to see this triumph of his son. Peter Ilich did not forget who it was that had given him his first chance to study music.

A festival cantata written to open the Polytechnic Exhibition in Moscow was performed early in June 1872. Then Tchaikovsky was off like an eager schoolboy to spend a month with his sister and her family at Kamenka.

Kamenka had already become a second home for the composer. It was a quiet vacation spot where he could rest his tired city nerves, a haven where he could take his hurt pride and his bruised ego when the critics became too harsh.

On their part, the family at Kamenka looked forward every year with increasing pleasure to the visits of Uncle Petia. Sasha mothered him along with her own brood, enjoyed his talk of travel and life in the city, played duets and talked music with him. Leo took him hunting, something of an ordeal for the composer, who could never stand the thought of death and turned faint at the sight of blood. Leo's brother Nicholas discussed literature and politics and garden flowers with him in the book-lined study where the elder Davydov had shut himself away from the annoyances of everyday living.

As for the children of Sasha and Leo, they were always standing at the gate looking down the road for hours for Uncle Petia's carriage to appear. When he did arrive, they descended upon him like a swarm of bees, kissing and hugging him, and poking his pockets playfully to look for the presents he always brought with him.

Bob, the fair-haired and charming, would be dancing up and down on his stout legs. Yuri would be perched high in a tree, a self-appointed lookout. Anna and Vera, arm in arm, would be walking up and down, up and down, venturing as far as the road when no one noticed. Tatiana, the exquisite oldest daughter, would be sitting pensively on the step, her eyes clouded with those dreamy thoughts which Uncle Petia and all the rest about her would have so liked to fathom.

The first evening of his visit in the summer of 1872 was, as usual, in the style of a festival, with Uncle Petia playing waltzes for the family and neighbors to dance to, and Leo Davydov acting the part of host in grand style with fine wines and the best meats and cheeses from the farm's stores. There was laughter and joking, and talk far into the night between sister and brother when the rest had gone to bed.

There was always so much to talk over. How was Anatol getting along? The boy should get married and settle down, now that he had such a good job. And Modeste. What luck was he having with his writing? Modeste, bless him, was almost as much a problem as Petia himself. Both of them restless and homeless. As for Hippolite, he seemed happy enough. And father, how was he taking Uncle Peter's recent death? What a crusty old soldier Uncle Peter had been! And he had lived a long life when one considered his wounds. But still, these things were a sorrow.

"Why don't you get married, Petia?" Sasha asked suddenly.

As usual, Peter Ilich's eyes clouded over unhappily. "Please, Sasha. I am not the type for marriage. My work is all I need. A clever woman would frighten me to death. A stupid one would bore me. I am too set in my ways, I am afraid. Besides, I like this home. It is all I need."

Sasha shook her head. She knew better. Peter needed a home. It was not good for him to wander always from place to place, living in other people's lives.

Sometimes Grandmother Alexandra and Vera and Elizabeth would be at Kamenka, too. Tchaikovsky was always pleased when this was so; for they were interesting women with hundreds of stories to tell of the days when Grandfather Vassily Davydov, the Decembrist, was sent with his comrades to Siberia. Grandmother Alexandra had gone with her husband into exile, and Elizabeth had made many trips back and forth to visit her parents. Grandmother proudly wore a bracelet made of a link of the chain which her husband wore on his leg during the terrible trip into Siberia.

Best of all her stories, though, were those she told of the poet Pushkin. There was a grotto back of the house where Vassily Davydov, a very wealthy man, had enjoyed giving banquets for his friends. By the light of torch flares and candles, a hundred people at a time had eaten of wild game and drunk imported wines and liqueurs while the songs of the Ukraine were sung for them by the sons and daughters of the Davydov serfs. Pushkin, the dreamer of dreams, the singer of songs, was often a guest. It was not uncommon for him to join the peasant dancers and show them how the wild Cossack dances from the Don were done.

Sitting in the grotto with the fragile old lady who belonged to a past era, Tchaikovsky's thoughts returned again and again to Pushkin.

"It may have been right here that he wrote his stories of the Caucasus Mountains—right here in the grotto. And who knows, perhaps the plot of *Eugene Oniegin* came to him here, too. You know, little mother, I never sit in this grotto that I don't see Eugene Oniegin come swaggering up. But more often I see Tatiana, who must have been very like our own sweet child who bears her name. Tatiana—beautiful, poignantly beautiful, with the brooding sadness which often hangs over youth like clouds in a summer's sky. Her hair, her eyes, her exquisite hands—I see them."

"It would make an opera," suggested Mother Alexandra.

Years later Tchaikovsky wrote an opera based on the story of Tatiana and Oniegin. Before he completed it, he talked over a proposed change with his good friend Mother Alexandra. They sat all night in the grotto back of the house while the earnest old lady begged the composer not to change the story as Pushkin wrote it. The composer argued his point quite as earnestly. Dawn found them laughing like two children. Mother Alexandra had her way, and Tchaikovsky's opera, like Pushkin's poem, was worked out to its inevitable dénouement of tragic frustration.

Eugene Oniegin has been acclaimed by the world as Tchaikovsky's most successful music for the stage. It is the story of a beautiful, gentle, unworldly girl, ignorant of life, who in all her simplicity offers her love to a jaded man of the world. This man—"this arch-swaggerer Oniegin"—is merely amused, fails to understand the depth of the girl's feeling, wounds her deeply by advising her coldly not to throw her love before the next man she meets.

The opera opens at the home of Tatiana. She and her sister Olga are singing to the accompaniment of a harp while their mother and an old nurse make preserves in the garden. The peasants appear from the fields, carrying the last sheaf from the harvest. The delightful songs and dances to celebrate the garnering of the harvest make a memorable scene.

At this point, Olga's sweetheart Lensky arrives, bringing with him a friend, dandified Oniegin. Tatiana falls in love with the handsome Oniegin. That night she writes a letter, telling this new-found friend that she loves him. The letter scene is one of the most poignant of all Tchaikovsky's inspirations.

Oniegin meets Tatiana next day in the garden, coldly rejects her love, tells her she is a foolish little country girl, leaves her crushed and tragic.

The second act opens on a ballroom scene. The music is gay and brilliant at first, but soon sounds an ominous tone. Oniegin persists in flirting with Olga. Lensky, unable to endure the situation, challenges his friend to a duel. The whole thing has blown up over nothing. Oniegin is actually sorry for his actions. But the accepted code of honor forces the two

WALTZ FROM "EUGENE ONIEGIN"

to take up pistols. Lensky is killed, and Oniegin, appalled by the tragic affair, becomes a wanderer in foreign lands.

Years elapse. Oniegin has returned home. He is present at a fashionable reception in St. Petersburg. There he meets a beautiful woman, wife of Prince Gremin. He is astounded to discover that the clever, bewitching Princess is none other than the little country girl Tatiana grown up.

Oniegin, the egoist, cannot imagine that events of the years following Tatiana's declaration of love for him can have changed her feeling. He falls in love in his turn and begs her to leave her husband. Tatiana, who respects and honors the

Prince, refuses. Oniegin is left desolate on the stage as the curtain falls.

The opera contains many graceful and brilliant dance melodies. One of these is a waltz, the inevitable romantic melody in three-four time which Tchaikovsky could never resist.

Before Tchaikovsky left Kamenka in 1872 he began his Second Symphony in C minor, Opus 17. The folk-songs which he heard everywhere that summer—sung by workmen at the house, by women working in the gardens around Kamenka, by the peasant children at the village fair—permeate this symphony to such an extent that the composer's contemporaries dubbed it the Ukrainian Symphony. It has also been called "the crane symphony," too, because of the beautiful folk-song "The Crane" which he skillfully elaborated to form the finale.

Hor - ses' hoofs raise dust on high.

17

$\mathcal{I}$n July of 1872, Tchaikovsky said good-by to his sister's household and started for Kiev, where he visited the twins. Then, taking Modeste with him, he set off by diligence for Nizy, where Kondratiev lived. On the return trip, the two brothers were to travel together as far as the town of Voroshba, where Peter Ilich planned to branch off to Ussovo and Modeste was to continue to Kiev.

They traveled as usual by post—the system in use before the railroads came, by which at regular stages of his journey the traveler was supplied with fresh horses for his carriage. Between Sumy and Voroshba the horses were to be changed at an inn provided with stables. Modeste and Peter prepared to enjoy a good lunch while they waited for the change to be made at the Post House. The meal was good, and the brothers ordered the best wines the house afforded. The innkeeper, who was also the master of the Post service, decided that such good customers would be profitable to keep around for a few days. What better way to keep them than to say that there were no fresh horses available, that his guests would have to wait for the tired ones to rest up? So it was done.

But Peter Ilich and Modeste were nineteenth-century Russians, and Peter had not worked in the bureaucratic Ministry of Justice for nothing. He detected an old dodge, and the wine gave him courage.

"Whom do you think you are talking to?" he demanded.

Modeste smiled to himself when the Post Master replied that he had not the slightest idea who Peter Ilich was and cared even less.

"Now what?" whispered Modeste wickedly.

"Let me see your report book, Innkeeper. I wish to write down my complaint." Tchaikovsky spoke as if he were a king who had just signed the order for the Prime Minister's beheading.

But the Post Master also was a nineteenth-century Russian, and he knew a bluff when he saw one. He brought the register and handed it over with a shrug of the shoulders.

The spirit of mischief entered Tchaikovsky at this point. Instead of writing his real name, which would have meant nothing whatever to the Post official, he wrote down "Prince Volkonsky, Page-in-Waiting."

The landlord took one look at the signature and turned pale.

"Ay, ya, yay!" he cried and rushed from the room.

In less than fifteen minutes horses had been found and hitched to the coach. The landlord and Post Master was bowing and scraping before the supposed prince and attendant on the Tsar, begging his pardon a thousand times, explaining over and over again that the head hostler had been severely reprimanded for not having reported that a pair of horses had just been unhitched from a coach returned from a short journey.

Laughing wildly over this comic incident, the brothers proceeded on their way to Voroshba. When they arrived, they found that a part of the joke had been on them. In the hustle and bustle of leave-taking, Tchaikovsky had left his pocketbook at the inn, with his passport and all his money and his papers in it.

"There is nothing for it but to send this carriage back and have the driver bring me the pocketbook," Tchaikovsky decided. "How much money do you have, Modi?"

Modeste had a few coins, just enough to pay for the extra trip to the inn. The coachman was duly dispatched. Modeste, in the meantime, caught his own train to Kiev.

Tchaikovsky's troubles were not over. The inn at Voroshba, where he had to spend the night while he waited for the coachman to return, was infested with rats, mice, and various other small game with which Russian inns of his day abounded. "He waged war all night with these pests, which ran over his bed and made a hideous noise," Modeste wrote of the incident in his memoirs.

Next day, the coachman returned to say that the landlord at the Post House would not trust the Prince's pocketbook to him, that the Prince must return for it himself. There was nothing for it but to make the tiresome trip back, and Tchaikovsky raged at himself every mile of the way. This surely was the Post official's way of getting even; for he must have looked inside the wallet and discovered that he was dealing with no prince but an impecunious young professor of music.

Arrived at the Post House, however, Tchaikovsky saw at a glance that he had done the landlord a grievous injustice, for the papers and money were undisturbed, and the man seemed to harbor no suspicion that his former guest was not a prince of the royal blood. Tchaikovsky was deeply grateful and inquired the name of the honest landlord.

"Tchaikovsky" was the reply—which sent the composer out of the inn with red ears. So the man had known all along that the prince story was a fabrication!

When Tchaikovsky reached Ussovo, he told the story of his mishap to Shilovsky, who laughed until the tears rolled down his cheeks. "The funny thing about it all—" he managed to gasp out; "the funny thing, Peter Ilich, is that I know that man, and his name really *is* Tchaikovsky!"

Back in Moscow, Tchaikovsky plunged headlong into work again. In an incredibly short time he turned out the incidental music to Ostrovsky's fairy tale *Snegourotchka* ("The Snow Maiden" or "Little Snow White"). Almost before the ink dried on the paper, he was jotting down notes for the symphonic fantasy *The Tempest*. This second masterpiece of program music, suggested by Shakespeare's play of the same name, was completed in the summer of 1873 and published as Opus 18.

The next two years were years of constant travel when he was not performing his duties at the Conservatory; of incessant composing wherever he was. *The Tempest* was orchestrated. When it was performed by the Musical Society in November, with great success, Tchaikovsky was already at work on his Quartet No. 2, in F major, Opus 22. Very soon he undertook another opera, *Vakoula the Smith*, based on one of Gogol's stories, *Christmas Night*.

A certain amount of comedy attended the writing of this opera. It was to be entered in a contest sponsored by the St. Petersburg Conservatory. Tchaikovsky not only misunderstood the date of closing and wrote the opera a year ahead of time, but also forgot that the manuscripts were supposed to be submitted anonymously and wrote his name on the cover. The judges laughed together at what they called "the mystery of who wrote Tchaikovsky's manuscript," but awarded him the prize in spite of everything, for his opera was far and away the best submitted.

Six Piano Pieces, Opus 21, and *Six Songs*, Opus 25, took form under Tchaikovsky's busy pen, and all the while an amazing work was taking form in his mind—his *Concerto* for piano, in B flat minor, Opus 23.

He played this composition on Christmas Eve in 1874 for Nicholas Rubinstein. Though he had had misgivings about presenting this work for Rubinstein's criticism, he was totally unprepared for the actual reception of his work. Rubinstein listened in cold silence to the first movement, and at the end of the last movement a torrent of abusive criticism poured from him. The concerto was bad technically, it could not be played—in fact, it was no credit to Tchaikovsky or to the institution with which he was associated.

Wrapping up his music, Tchaikovsky stalked from the room, went immediately to his study and erased Rubinstein's name from the dedication page, replacing it with that of Hans von Bülow. The composer was right in his judgment. Bülow gave the concerto prominent place at nearly all his concerts, and it was invariably received with enthusiasm. In 1878, Rubinstein realized the mistake he had made and, by studying the work and playing it brilliantly both in Russia and abroad, healed the wound he had inflicted on his friend.

The concerto opens with a majestic four-bar prelude. Then the piano is heard in a series of crashing chords while the orchestra plays a melody which sings victoriously throughout this vigorous movement:

The first subject proper of this movement is a plaintive air which Tchaikovsky heard sung by blind beggars at a fair:

The second subject consists of two melodies, the first played by the woodwinds and the piano:

The second melody is heard briefly, played by the violins:

The second movement contains a tender lullaby-like melody, announced by the flutes:

The finale (see next page) is robust and colorful, a brilliant theme suggesting a spirited victory dance of warriors returned home to celebrate.

The second melody of the *finale* speaks of tenderness and hope, the good things of life:

It is perhaps the robust, hopeful quality of the music of the concerto that has endeared it to Americans, who took it to their hearts at its world premiere, when Bülow played it in Boston in Music Hall on October 25, 1875, with Benjamin Lang conducting.

Teaching, traveling, fighting off fits of depression and loneliness, Tchaikovsky managed to get through the year 1875. No matter what his inner conflict, however, his pen did not cease to move across the music pages.

A serenade for violin, Opus 26; *Six Songs*, Opus 27; *Six Songs*, Opus 28; Quartet No. 3, Opus 30; and the first sketches for the *Swan Lake Ballet*. So much work would mean only one thing: Peter Ilich had reached some crisis in his life.

One brief amusing scene remained for the composer to play before he entered on the act which was tragedy. This amusing episode attended the coming of the French composer Saint-Saëns to Moscow. He and Tchaikovsky were immediately attracted to each other. They talked over their common likes and dislikes, discovered that both were passionate devotees of the art of the ballet.

"I have always had a foolish desire to dance—actually dance —in a ballet," confessed Saint-Saëns, coloring a little and laughing apologetically.

"But so have I!" exclaimed Tchaikovsky. "I have never before told anyone, but whenever I see a stage full of dancers leaping and whirling, the urge to put on slippers and costume and join them is almost too great." Tchaikovsky laughed in his turn.

That is what gave these two the idea of writing a little ballet together.

What is more, they persuaded amused Nicholas Rubinstein to play the music of the ballet for them while they danced. The spectacle of forty-year-old Saint-Saëns and thirty-five-year-old Tchaikovsky dancing the story of *Pygmalion and Galatea*, with Rubinstein acting the dual role of orchestra and audience, must have set the gods on Olympus laughing.

I saw my bride by Fate's de - cree

18

The years 1876 and 1877 were fateful years for Tchaikovsky. Two women entered his life—one whom he never once spoke to, and one whom he married. Both affected the future course of his life.

The first of these women was Nadejda von Meck, widow of the railroad builder and owner, mother of eleven children, possessor of many fine estates and homes, manager with her son of an enormous fortune. Madame von Meck was a forceful, clever woman, who had not always been wealthy. She had directed the energies of her engineer husband into audacious and prosperous undertakings; she had been willing to live on a few cents a day while the bold plans she laid for her husband's future matured. Driving, urging, planning, denying herself luxuries, she had worn herself out in the battle. When her husband died, she retired into the little world of her family, seeing as few people from the outer world as was possible for a woman of her many affairs. She kept control of one of her railroads and all her farm estates, managing them efficiently from her desk at home by employing her son Vladimir as go-between in dealings with others.

The von Mecks were a family to excite respect in Russia and even abroad, where most Russians were supposed to wear nothing but bearskins, eat nothing but tallow candles, hunt wolves as their only relaxation. The story is told of Nadejda's beloved Vladimir, talented businessman with a decided inclination for the dramatic, that when one of the von Meck railroads needed a loan he went to Paris to interview the international bankers of the powerful House of Rothschild. This house was so wealthy and so powerful that it dealt not with individuals but with governments. But the von Mecks of Russia were a family powerful enough to be a government, the Rothschilds reasoned, and granted Vladimir an interview. However, to impress him properly with the importance of their organization, they sent a messenger to his hotel to ask how many secretaries the Russian client intended to bring with him.

"Why do you want to know?" Vladimir asked shrewdly.

"We should like to know how many chairs to provide for the audience," was the bland reply.

Vladimir's eyes twinkled. "How many secretaries does Mr. Rothschild have?"

The messenger was somewhat taken aback by being questioned in his turn, but saw no reason not to reply. "Six," was the answer.

"I have twelve," said Vladimir without so much as a quiver of his eyelashes.

When the messenger had gone, Vladimir scurried around looking up friends living in Paris. This was not too difficult a task, since all the wealthy Russians spent much of their time abroad in the French capital.

Next morning Vladimir, dressed carefully in correct morn-

ing attire, walked into the offices of the Rothschilds. Behind
him walked his bookkeeper, and behind the bookkeeper
walked eleven faithful friends, who performed their duties as
secretaries—that is, the duty of rising when Vladimir rose,
sitting when he sat—faultlessly. The von Mecks got the loan.

Such were the von Mecks—brilliant, arrogant, audacious.
Nadejda, however, was ill. Toward the end of her life she
developed tuberculosis. Besides, she was the victim of nineteenth-century ideas about women: they were not supposed
to think like men, they were not supposed to manage huge
estates and railroads openly, and, when they reached forty,
they were considered old. A mother of eleven children was
thought to be ready for a lace cap and a seat in the chimney
corner. Nadejda was anything but ready for the fireside seat,
but she was too ill and too shy to fight the opinions of the
world. This proud, arrogant woman chose instead to become
a virtual recluse, managing the affairs of her family with the
firm hand of a tyrant, turning to music as her one relaxation
and consolation.

When Nicholas Rubinstein saw that his brilliant professor
of harmony was falling into a serious state of melancholy he
decided that something should be done. Knowing that no
matter how modestly Tchaikovsky lived, he was always in
debt, principally because he constantly gave money to members of his family temporarily out of suits with fortune and to
any friend or acquaintance who held out a palm, Rubinstein
concluded that the whole trouble was lack of money. Therefore, he reasoned, the most practical way to help his friend
was to get more money for him. That is why he took the
manuscript of *The Tempest* under his arm and made his way
to the imposing house where the widow von Meck lived.

"I have something for you to listen to." He spoke without

preamble to the rustling black figure that swept so imperiously down the staircase into the music-room with its gilt and plush and crowded, expensive fussiness.

Nicholas Rubinstein was one of the few people outside the family circle admitted to Nadejda's home. He was admitted because he treated the imperious recluse as man to man. They understood each other, these two tyrannical natures. Each was used to bending all others' wills to theirs. Nadejda arranged marriages for her children without consulting them; Rubinstein arranged the financial affairs of his protégés.

Without a word Nadejda rustled into an adjoining room. Rubinstein seated himself at the piano and played, knowing Madame von Meck's habit of listening to music when she was entirely alone. Hers was a strange, unhealthily shy nature, emotional and not given to restraint. Hers also was a cautious mind, careful not to give way to emotion for others to see.

When the last note of the music depicting the love of Miranda and Ferdinand had died away in the dusk of the music-room, Nadejda opened the door. Even in the half-light Rubinstein could see that her cheeks were flushed and her eyes shining with excitement.

"Whose is it?" Nadejda's voice was hushed, as if the woman were making an effort to control it.

"Composed by Peter Ilich Tchaikovsky. A teacher at the Conservatory. A genius." Rubinstein looked at the widow through languid, half-closed eyelids. If she saw the wicked twinkle in the blue eyes, Nadejda paid no attention.

"What do you want?" Nadejda was nothing if not to the point. With her practical and somewhat disillusioned view of life she knew that few came to play sweet music for her for nothing.

"I want you to order something from Tchaikovsky now and

then—some trifling composition—and pay him for it. He needs money, more than the Conservatory can afford to pay."

"If I do, you understand that this—this Peter Ilich Tchaikovsky—must not try to see me. This will be a purely impersonal affair. You understand that, Nicholas Rubinstein?"

Rubinstein bowed his ironic bow. "Perfectly, Madame."

"Very well. I shall communicate with him."

Thus ended the interview which was to have such far-reaching consequences for the composer. From this time on Madame von Meck interested herself in Tchaikovsky and his music, eventually becoming passionately fond of both the composer and his work. They kept up an enormous correspondence, speaking out freely about their personal problems, family life, opinions on music—in short, whatever they might have talked about had they met; and Tchaikovsky always referred to Nadejda as his "beloved friend" or his "best friend." By mutual consent, however, the two never spoke one word face to face, and met by chance only on two or three occasions, when they merely nodded in passing.

As a matter of fact Nadejda had heard a great deal of Tchaikovsky from Joseph Kotek, a violinist who had studied theory with the composer at the Conservatory. This young musician was employed in her household partly as a teacher to her children, partly just to bring to her the music she loved. Nadejda played the piano well, and liked to have someone to join her in interpreting new scores. It was not unusual for her to hire a whole ensemble or concert orchestra if she wished to hear a new work without going to a public performance. It was Kotek who carried to Tchaikovsky her first letter with the order for a piano-and-violin arrangement. Two months later another commission came, and another letter. Thus began the strange friendship.

Though Rubinstein's diagnosis of his friend's melancholy was not entirely correct—for, to him, loneliness and an increasing conviction that art could not thrive in the ugliness and disorder of the life about him were its basis—the increased income from Nadejda's fat purse was a tremendous help to him. For one thing, the added commissions kept him busy, and as always, Tchaikovsky could come near to forgetting his troubles in work.

With 1876 came the composition of some of the composer's greatest works. These included *The Seasons* (Opus 37), a group of charming piano interpretations of the moods evoked by the months of the year. Tchaikovsky's sensitive feeling for mood, for the emotional content of experiences, is well illustrated in these simple pieces for the piano. *March* is the song of the lark. *July* is a reaper's song. *October* is sad, for summer is at an end, and winter's gaunt cold will succeed the harvest.

"March," "July," and "October" from "The Seasons"

Francesca da Rimini, inspired by the gloomy "Inferno" section of Dante's epic *Divina Commedia* constitutes—with

The Tempest and *Romeo and Juliet*—the third of a trilogy of the most emotional program compositions of all time. In these symphonic works Tchaikovsky makes his bow to the world as the first major representative of the school of psychological realism. As Turgeniev, Dostoyevsky, and Tolstoi in the realm of literature, so Tchaikovsky in the realm of music was striving to give expression to the spiritual life of man. What he found in man's experience was seldom happy, often ugly; therefore his works contain much that is tragic. But—what is sometimes forgotten—they always resound with a passionate call to a better life.

Perhaps the most delightful of all his compositions of 1876 was the *Swan Lake Ballet*, written on commission of the Moscow Directorate of Theaters. The story of the ballet is based on a German legend:

A young prince, Siegfried, has been ordered to choose a bride at a banquet to be given for the most attractive girls of the realm. On the eve of the banquet he sees a flock of swans and sets out to follow them. The swans settle down beside a lake, and as darkness comes on, the prince is amazed to see them change into beautiful young girls. One is Princess Odette, who tells him that she and her companions have been bewitched by a magician and forced to take the form of swans by day, returning to their human shape only at night.

Siegfried and Odette fall in love, and the princess tells him that he has it in his power to release her from the spell if he will always love her and no other. Siegfried gladly promises, but is tricked into betraying his promise by the magician, who has brought to the banquet his own daughter, Odelia, in the form of Odette. Siegfried, supposing Odelia to be his beloved Odette, chooses her joyfully to be his bride and thus quite innocently plays his love false. The real Odette, rather than remain in her swan-state forever, waits for night and throws herself, a mortal maiden, into the lake. When Siegfried learns of his tragic error he follows his loved one in death.

Tchaikovsky's music is both delicate and eerie. The dim, misty lake scene, the unearthly beauty of the swan maidens, the half-dreaming love mood of the young prince, the wood-land shyness of the princess—these are moods and scenes called up in the rich melodies and colorful orchestral style of the dances.

The Spanish Dance from the banquet scene is in the scintillating rhythm of the bolero:

The finale displays the quicksilver quality which pervades the entire score.

It was in this year, too, that Tchaikovsky composed that most "national" of compositions, *Marche Slave*. Surely he was remembering Fanny Dürbach's stories of the ancient peoples who loved barbaric color and ceremony, who valued the ancient harp more than the sword, who would rather have the Norseman Rurik rule them than bother to rule themselves, when he set down the opening chords of this famous work—printed on the following page.

Moderato. In modo di marcia funebre.

Nicholas Rubinstein congratulated himself; for it seemed that all was well with Peter Ilich who moved about in society meeting famous people. Among them was Tolstoi, whose interest in Tchaikovsky's works surprised and pleased him.

"Never in the whole course of my life," he wrote in his diary, "did I feel so flattered, never so proud of my creative power, as when Leo Tolstoi, sitting by my side, listened to my *Andante* [First String Quartet] while the tears streamed down his face."

It was the folk-song theme in the *Andante* that pleased the great writer. Here, as in the first Piano Concerto, the choruses in the operas *Mazeppa*, *Eugene Oniegin*, and *The Enchantress*, and the finales of the Second and the Fourth symphonies, Tchaikovsky drew a vigorous optimism from the songs of the people. He often spoke of folk-songs as the "reed" from which he grew a "luxurious tree." That is why his melodies have remained so close to the common people of all nations. Tolstoi and Tchaikovsky exchanged several letters on the subject of folk-music, and the Count took the trouble to send Tchaikovsky a collection gathered from the peasants in his district.

The following year Tchaikovsky composed six of his greatest songs (Opus 38). The first of these was *Don Juan's Serenade*, to words by Tolstoi. It is a rugged, wild Iberian melody, indicating the artist Tchaikovsky's ability to step out of his "Russianism" to create the mood of another land (the Iberian Peninsula of Southwest Europe, now Spain and Portugal).

In this year Tchaikovsky in his capacity of critic went to Bayreuth to attend the Wagner festival, and liked neither the festival nor the music. His impressions were not improved when he called on Wagner and the genius of Bayreuth refused to see the genius from Russia.

Tchaikovsky wrote his impression to Modeste:

"Bayreuth has left me with disagreeable recollections, although my artistic ambition was flattered more than once. It appears I am by no means as unknown in Western Europe as I believed. The disagreeable recollections are raised by the uninterrupted bustle in which I was obliged to take part. It finally came to an end on Thursday. After the last notes of the Götterdämmerung, I felt as though I had been let out of prison. The Nibelungen may be actually a magnificent work, but it is certain that there never was anything so endlessly and wearisomely spun out."

Even to the members of his family Tchaikovsky seemed in the best of spirits. A letter to Modeste about this time is written in light, playful mood:

"Honored Mr. Modeste Ilich,—I do not know if you still remember me. I am your brother and a professor at the Moscow Conservatory. I have also composed a few things; operas, symphonies, overtures, etc. Once upon a time you honored me by your personal acquaintance. Last year we were abroad together and spent a time which I shall never forget. You used frequently to write me long and interesting letters. Now all this seems like a beautiful dream. . . ."

No one suspected that Tchaikovsky was tormented with loneliness and doubts of himself, that he was finding his teaching more and more a bore, and feeling sometimes that no one cared either for the composer or for his art. Tchaikovsky, remembering the unfortunate outcome of his engagement to Désirée Artôt, was careful to tell none that he had decided to follow Sasha's often repeated advice and get married. A wife to look after him was what he needed, he said to himself. Not a brilliant woman; of such he was afraid. He was sure, for instance, that a few moments' conversation face to face with Nadejda von Meck would throw him into a panic— his intellect would prove to be inferior to hers. In this Tchaikovsky shared the nineteenth-century man's horror of the clever woman. His wife must not be too well educated, must not know a great deal about music, must have no interest but cooking and cleaning for her husband. And in this approach to the problem of marriage lay a dangerous pitfall. And when, later, he had plunged into this pitfall, he climbed back to sanity and peace only by superhuman effort, and to the end of his life he bore the scars of the wounds made by the folly which overtook him in the year 1877.

Spring was in the air. Along the streets of Moscow the trees were beginning to show the fresh young leaves, and apple blossoms made the evenings sweet in the countryside. Everyone who could afford a carriage was driving out to Petrovsky Park to hear the nightingales. Young and gay as the spring itself, pretty, ignorant Antonina Milyukov came tripping on light feet into Tchaikovsky's life. She wrote him a letter saying that she had been a pupil in one of his classes. Tchaikovsky could not remember her, and he forgot the incident until another letter came. He himself in later years told his good friend Kashkin how it came about that in the midst of the most strenuous work on his great opera *Eugene Oniegin* he dropped his pen and went to call on the writer of those letters.

For weeks and months the composer had been living with the tragic characters of his opera, swaggering Eugene Oniegin and shy, sensitive, beautiful Tatiana. One scene in the drama drew him like a magnet—ardent young Tatiana pouring out her love in a letter to Oniegin. The garden scene, in which the world-weary Oniegin, unable to grasp the sincerity of Tatiana's confession, wounds the sensitive girl by calling her bold and silly, roused Tchaikovsky's artistic wrath.

"I became so accustomed to the image of Tatiana," the composer told Kashkin, "that she and all that surrounded her became alive for me. I loved Tatiana and was hotly indignant with Oniegin, who seemed to me a cold, heartless fop."

Thus it was that Tchaikovsky, lost to the practical affairs of the world while he lived in the none-too-healthful atmosphere of a nineteenth-century romance, viewed Antonina's second letter through distorted lenses. She reproached him bitterly for not answering her first letter. Tchaikovsky immediately envisaged himself as a cold, cruel Oniegin and Antonina as a crushed Tatiana. He must not act as Oniegin had! He determined to marry the stranger who declared that she could not live without him. And marry her he did, without a word to any of his colleagues in the Conservatory.

This marriage lasted only a few weeks. No one ever knew the complete story of the tragic affair. One thing is sure, however: Tchaikovsky had a complete nervous breakdown, which threatened his sanity. Careful nursing by his brothers, money from Nadejda to take him for a rest cure abroad, his never-ceasing struggle to rise out of his trouble—these things helped to save him. The real cure was designated by Tchaikovsky himself in a letter to his "beloved friend."

"I have emerged from the strife victorious. . . . I was saved by work. . . ."

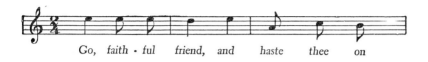

Go, faith - ful friend, and haste thee on

19

<big>T</big>chaikovsky never suspected
that his marriage brought suf-
fering to any other than himself, his wife, and the anxious
members of his family. Suffering, like happiness, can be
selfish. The composer was blind to the fact that his rash action
had wounded proud, sensitive Nadejda. She wore a mask for
the world to see most of the time. Behind that mask, as her
letters revealed now and then, was a woman eager for life, a
woman who might have come out of her seclusion if there
had been one to hold out a welcoming hand.

It would have been easy enough to break off relations with
the composer; for idle tongues were spreading malicious rumors, not the least of which was the story that Tchaikovsky
was hopelessly mad. Popular opinion would have upheld the
widow if she had washed her hands of the whole unpleasant
matter. Nadejda, however, was never one to conform to popular opinion. Whatever battle she had with herself, she fought
out alone. If the mask slipped from her face for a moment, it

was in the privacy of her own suite. When she wrote to the composer in Clarens, Switzerland, where Anatol had taken him after his breakdown, her letter voiced no reproaches; instead it contained money and the information that she had taken it upon herself to give Tchaikovsky an annual pension of 6000 rubles ($3000).

A crushing weight rolled off Peter Ilich. Tired and ill, with money enough to pay for only six weeks' stay in the Swiss town on Lake Geneva, he had been close to despair. The thought of returning to the Conservatory, to Moscow where evil tongues were wagging, had made him sick at heart. Nadejda had saved him. At last he was free, free to move about at will, free to compose whenever, wherever, whatever he chose.

A grateful letter of thanks was sent off to Nadejda, and Tchaikovsky packed his bags and set forth on his wanderings. Clarens, usually so quiet and peaceful, was oppressive to him because of the hundreds of political refugees fleeing from the persecutions of Tsar Alexander II. Russia's volcano was erupting again. The country was at war with Turkey, a costly war which ended a year later in disaster and disgrace for the Tsar's foreign policy.

Though Turkey was defeated, the Treaty of San Stefano was but a short triumph for Russia. Great Britain and Austria-Hungary feared the power of the Russian Bear, decided it was time to dull his claws, met at Berlin and insisted that the Tsar disgorge some of his gains in the Turkish war. Thus humiliated abroad, the government at home lost face. In its anger it lashed out right and left at those who dared to criticize.

While he was fighting the difficult battle with his nerves, Tchaikovsky traveled. Moving from place to place seemed to bring him some relief. He went first to Florence, then to

Rome and Venice. Next thing he was in Vienna. Before long he was back in Venice. Milan came next, and then San Remo, which held him longer than the other towns.

He wrote Nadejda from San Remo in January 1878, describing its beauties:

"The situation of San Remo is truly enchanting. The little town lies on a hill, and is closely packed together. The lower town consists almost exclusively of hotels, which are all overcrowded. . . . Today, without exaggeration, we are having summer weather. The sun was almost unbearable, even without an overcoat. Everywhere one sees olive trees, palms, oranges, lemons, heliotrope, jasmine—in short, it is gloriously beautiful."

Then quite unexpectedly for one who had been dreading thoughts of home he wrote:

"And yet—shall I tell you or not? When I walk by the sea I am seized with a desire to go home and pour out all my yearnings and agitations in a letter to you, or to Toly [his brother Anatol]. Why? Why should a simple Russian landscape, a walk through our homely villages and woods, a tramp over the fields and steppes at sunset, inspire me with such an intense love of nature that I throw myself on the earth and give myself up to the enchantment with which all these humble things can fill me? Why? I only observe the fact without attempting to explain it."

But perhaps this admission of his longing for home was not so unusual after all. Peter Ilich was himself again, or at least very nearly so.

"I assure you," he went on, "that neither the palms, nor the oranges, nor the beautiful blue sea, nor the mountains make the impression upon me which they might be expected to do. Consolation, peace, well-being, I can only draw from within.

The success of the Symphony, the consciousness that I am writing something good, will reconcile me tomorrow to all the friction and worry of previous days."

That symphony, that "something good," was Tchaikovsky's Fourth Symphony, in F minor, Opus 36. It was dedicated to "My Best Friend," who was Nadejda—she who had inspired it.

In a letter to his patron, Tchaikovsky revealed that this work, to which he often referred as "our symphony," had a program. In it definite thoughts and moods and ideas had been given musical form. He characterized the first phrase, that chilling and sharply menacing opening, as the voice of Fate.

"This force," he said, "is inescapable and invincible."

The sense of hopeless despair grows stronger and more poignant, and the main theme of the first movement is one of the most mournful of melodies.

And then "O joy! A sweet and tender dream enfolds me."

"Here is happiness."

"It is but a dream. Fate wakens us roughly."

"So all life is but a continual alternation between grim truth and fleeting dreams of happiness. There is no haven." Thus the composer summed up the program of the first movement.

The plaintive little Russian melody in the second movement he described as "the melancholy that comes in the evening when we sit alone, and weary of work, we try to read, but the book falls from our hands. Memories crowd in upon us."

In the fourth movement he revealed that he subscribed to the Tolstoian principle of looking for good in the common people. "Go to the people," Tchaikovsky wrote to explain the mood of this movement. "See—they know how to make the best of their time, how to give themselves up to pleasure! A peasant festival is depicted." The finale is actually a skillful treatment of the folk-song "A Birch Tree in the Wood."

It is significant that Tchaikovsky, whose dissatisfaction with life gave rise to mournful and tragic music, who often asserted the idea of an inexorable fate preventing man from living freely and joyously, nearly always ended by asserting that man must and should struggle against this fate. In his music as in his life, the idea of struggle toward something better was ever present.

Beginning with the Fourth Symphony, this determined struggle toward life and light becomes very evident. In the Fourth, he reached a sort of compromise solution to the problem with the assertion that though life is difficult it is nevertheless possible to live. In the Fifth and Sixth sym-

phonies his struggle worked itself out to subtly different con-
clusions. In the Fifth, he was more optimistic, asserting that

PIMPINELLA

it is not only possible but necessary to live. With the Sixth he
found a partially negative answer: It is no longer possible to
live. Nevertheless, one cries out against this fate. One is
defiant!

Having told Nadejda of this "program" for the Fourth,

Tchaikovsky went on to say that, at best, words can give but an imperfect idea of music, since literature and music are separate arts, and what is possible for one is not possible for the other. Music is emotion, pure and simple, is what he said in effect. It can neither delineate a scene (as a picture can) nor describe or narrate events (as poetry and prose can). "Where words cease, there music begins," he quoted from Heine.

The composer was listening to folk-songs in Italy just as he always did in Russia. *Pimpinella*, No. 6 of Opus 30, was a melody he took down from a street singer. (See page 192.)

In Florence he heard a handsome boy singing a song as much a growth of the Italian soil as the red wine in raffia-covered bottles. He noted it down and used it as the middle section of the piano piece which is No. 12 of Opus 40. In Rome he stayed in a hotel next to the Cuirassiers' barracks. Every morning he was roused along with the soldiers by a spirited bugle call. This call went into the opening phrases of the *Capriccio Italienne*, Opus 45.

Meanwhile he worked at *Eugene Oniegin*, that opera which in his case had served as the instrument of fate, the fate which Tchaikovsky believed kept mankind from being happy. Tatiana had tricked the composer into his tragic marriage; yet he loved his beautiful heroine none the less.

When the opera was finished he wrote Nadejda (February 1878):

"I am in rose-colored mood. Glad the opera is finished, glad spring is at hand, glad I am well and free, glad to feel safe from unpleasant meetings [Here he referred to the fact that his family and friends had made satisfactory arrangements with Antonina, so that she would not trouble Peter Ilich further] . . . and to be conscious that I may eventually perfect my art. I trust this feeling is no self-deception, but a just appreciation of my powers."

In the spring he came home, and a pretty time for a homecoming it was! Typhus was raging in St. Petersburg, diphtheria and smallpox in Moscow. The cholera was merely waiting for fall and the raw swampy mists. The spring thaw had set in. Rivers were flooding, and mud made the outskirts of the cities a series of quagmires. Frightened people were washing floors and furniture with carbolic acid; but, Nadejda complained in one of her letters to the composer, no one seemed to think of doing anything about the piles of refuse thrown carelessly from every kitchen and allowed to sour and fester under the spring sun.

Soon after his return, Nadejda issued to her protégé one of the strangest invitations on record. She would be glad, she wrote, if the composer would visit her country home of Brailov. She herself would not be there, she hastened to assure him.

Tchaikovsky was in seventh heaven at Brailov, a magnificent house with acres stretching away from it as far as the eye could see. Lilacs scented the air, and nightingales sang in the not-too-distant wood. A well-trained staff of servants had been instructed to make the composer at home. He was met at the station by a carriage from Brailov. The butler Marcel sat beside the coachman, and Tchaikovsky recorded, "His coat and hat were infinitely superior to mine, so that I felt quite embarrassed. . . ."

A silver samovar and a coffee pot with a spirit lamp steamed on the dining-room table, and the finest food had been prepared for the meal. The servants had had their instructions. They were careful to keep out of sight when the composer ate and afterward when he explored the library and music-room of the house.

Tchaikovsky lived on at Brailov for several weeks, like an Aladdin whose genie appeared when he rubbed the lamp. Every morning after having coffee, he strolled in the garden. Slipping through a little wooden door in the wall near the stable and jumping a ditch, he entered a forsaken garden which had formerly belonged to a monastery. In the green shade of wild trees and shrubs which had taken the place of the cultivated plants of the old monks, Tchaikovsky would sit for hours thinking out themes for his music.

The composer was to return many times to this luxurious retreat. Several of his finest works were completed there, notably the First Orchestral Suite, Opus 43, and the opera *Joan of Arc*. The bold, clear-cut nature of the music of this opera is illustrated in a simple melody in four-four time (see music on next page) .

In 1878, Tchaikovsky resigned his position at the Moscow Conservatory. From this time on these strange invitations of Nadejda's came more and more often. The composer became accustomed to his unusual vacations. A visit to Nadejda's town house in Moscow, when his hostess was abroad. Living at the small estate of Simaki, within easy walking distance of Brailov, where Nadejda herself was staying, and never a glimpse of his hostess. Accepting the gift of a vacation in Florence, in a villa furnished by his patron, within a stone's throw of her own villa, and only once meeting her as she passed by in her carriage.

In 1881, a celebration was held in Russia to salute a quarter

JOAN OF ARC

of a century of rule by Alexander II. There must have been those who did not think this reign anything to be jubilant over. The next year the Tsar was killed by a Nihilist bomb. Alexander III took the throne, and the inevitable arrests, persecutions, and suppressions followed.

Tchaikovsky found himself sighing over the days that were past. It was too late for the composer to understand the meaning of the social forces about him. He could only stand bewildered at the spectacle of two orders, the old and the new, girding for titanic struggle.

In his own life important changes were taking place. In 1880, kindly Father Ilya had died. Sasha was ill at Kamenka, painfully and incurably ill. Tatiana, the eldest daughter of the household, had reached out eagerly for life and gathered tragedy into her lovely hands. No amount of patience on Uncle Petia's part would take her mind from her melancholy thoughts. She did not understand his creed of struggle. She preferred to run away from life. So Kamenka had become a gloomy place, no longer the haven it had been for the composer.

And in 1881, Nicholas Rubinstein died. Tchaikovsky went to Paris when news came that the great artist was mortally ill, but he arrived too late. The sight of the imperious, proud Nicholas lying humbled by Death, "that flat-nosed horror" as Tchaikovsky always called it, was a terrible shock. In memory of this good friend and great artist, who lay so still with his powerful pianist's hands folded and quiet at last, Tchaikovsky wrote the Trio, Opus 50, for piano, violin, and cello.

In 1882, another opera based on a Pushkin poem was written—*Mazeppa*, a story of the time of Peter the Great. In 1883, the Suite No. 2 for orchestra, Opus 53, was composed.

The *Children's Songs*, Opus 54, were a sort of farewell wave of the hand to that most charming memory of Kamenka, the children standing at the gate waiting for Uncle Petia and his gifts. The "Waltz" (below on the left) might have been one that Uncle Petia played in the evening for the young people to dance to, and "The New Doll" (below on the right) was surely one of the gifts he brought.

There were many memories of Kamenka—droll in retrospect—that made a lump come into the composer's throat. The time that nervous Uncle Petia made plans to cut his visit short and go to Florence, where Nadejda had prepared the vacation villa for him. In the midst of excited preparations for the trip, robust Leo Davydov burst in to propose a wolf hunt as a proper send-off for a Russian about to leave for Italy. The year before, one of these hunts had sent Tchaikovsky to bed a sick man. Not wanting to appear a weak sister in Leo's eyes, however, he tried to seem enthusiastic.

"Splendid," he murmured faintly.

Leo was delighted, slapped him on the back heartily, boomed: "Wolf, fox, and wild goat! Ah! Of course, we may not have the luck to shoot goat. They're getting very scarce and shy."

Peter Ilich closed his eyes and prayed that the wolves might be even scarcer and shyer. He spent a restless night, next day carried his heavy gun for hours through the woods, finally stumbled home without wolf or goat or even rabbit, and was too ill to take his train.

Again at Kamenka, when Uncle Petia, entering into the pleasant life of the village, agreed to help his sister with the music in the village church. He and she, brother Anatol, and the pretty niece Tatiana, formed a vocal quartet to sing a hymn on St. Catherine's Day.

As a boy of ten, Peter Ilich told the family circle, he had often sung hymns in the St. Petersburg churches, where his voice had been considered remarkably sweet, and true. Rehearsals got under way, and everyone at home said the hymn sounded beautiful. But in church, Tatiana lost her head, forgot her notes, and led them all astray. Sasha and Anatol stopped in confusion, but Uncle Petia, always the complete professional, kept on singing alone. It was a mistake. The voice which had been all right at ten had become a typical "composer's voice." Uncle Petia croaked like a crow.

The year 1885 marked the end of the days at Kamenka. It was a milestone, too, in Tchaikovsky's artistic life. Like the chambered nautilus of the ocean floor, he moved forward as he grew, closing off the old chambers with their memories. In this year, he came out of the neurotic chamber of his shell and began to enjoy his fame.

Though the house be ver - y small and quaint,

20

When he was in Paris in 1884, the composer wrote Modeste a letter in which he said: "I can scarcely tell you, dear Modi, how wearisome the last few days have been—although I cannot say why. It proceeds chiefly from homesickness, the desire for a place of my own; and even the knowledge that I start for Russia tomorrow brings no satisfaction, *because I have no home anywhere.* . . . I must have a *home,* be it in Kamenka or Moscow. I cannot go on living the life of a wandering star. . . . Where will my home be?"

That is why, although he had begun to enjoy being famous, his enthusiasm was somewhat less than his friends thought it should be. In 1885, Hans von Bülow, who had in turn been an ardent disciple of both Wagner and Brahms and was entering upon his "Russian enthusiasm," came to St. Petersburg and directed a performance of Tchaikovsky's Third Suite, Opus 55. Bülow's genius in getting the most from an orchestra, particularly when his current favorite among composers was being featured, was united to the attractive and understandable character of the music. Tchaikovsky had never before had such a satisfying success; yet in the midst of the cheering and lionizing his mind kept reverting to thoughts of a home, a little hideaway where he could be a musical hermit.

Faithful servant Alexis was delegated to choose a place. Naturally, he selected his home village of Maidanovo, just north of the town of Klin, which lies close to Moscow on the railroad connecting with St. Petersburg.

Alexis took a furnished house on the banks of the Sestra River, a rather large place which had once belonged to a wealthy Russian family. When Tchaikovsky saw the neglected gardens and the uninspiring view he was disappointed, but concealed his feelings from Alexis, who was thoroughly delighted with everything.

So at last the composer had his home. He moved several times between 1885 and 1892, but always took houses in the neighborhood of Maidanovo and Klin, the village where he settled finally and became known to friends and villagers alike as "the hermit of Klin."

As soon as he was established at Maidanovo, he began to work on the symphonic composition *Manfred* based on Byron's poem. In spirit this orchestral work is akin to the Fourth and Fifth symphonies. It has a definite program, suggested by Balakirev:

The first part depicts bored, disillusioned Manfred's roamings in search of peace and happiness. The second part presents the Witch of the Alps, who appears to Manfred in the sunbow of a Swiss torrent. The third part, pastoral in nature, is a picture of the wholesome, simple life of the Alpine shepherds. The fourth part is a sort of demon frolic, during which the shade of Astarte, symbol of man's eternal striving

for ideal happiness, appears for a moment before Manfred
dies.

All unknown to Tchaikovsky, his friends were enjoying
many a jest at his expense. The composer, who thoroughly
disliked the practical affairs of life, had entrusted the furnish-
ing of his new home to Alexis. Alexis, good, ignorant old man
that he was, had set to work to buy beds, chairs, draperies,
and rugs, as well as kitchen and dining-room utensils and
dishes. His selection was the most hideous that could be
imagined. The old peasant thought them beautiful, and when
Tchaikovsky saw them he expressed complete satisfaction.
Tchaikovsky the artist in music was no artist otherwise.

The composer spoke proudly to friends who came to visit
him about "my dishes, my cook, my washerwoman, my furniture"—all pleased him equally. Privately, his friends agreed
that they were glad that these things and people were "his"
and not theirs. The cook plagued them especially, for she
turned out the most tasteless and meager meals, and guests
usually went away from the table hungry. They would be still
further annoyed that Tchaikovsky invariably sent congratula-
tions to the cook on her efforts.

His friends laughed too at the composer's own contribu-
tions to the furnishings: a clock which would not run and
two horses for which he had no need and which were got rid
of only with the greatest difficulty.

Tchaikovsky's only requirement, it seemed, was that
nothing in the household, having once been placed, should
be moved. If the portrait of Anton Rubinstein was hung on
the north wall of the living-room when he moved into a
house, woe betide the over-zealous servant who chanced to
move it to the south or the east or the west wall. Even when
he moved from place to place, he liked to have his pictures
and other belongings disposed about the new quarters in as

nearly as possible the same positions they had occupied in the old. Alexis watched over these details like a faithful bulldog, seeing to it that everything was as "the master wished it."

Tchaikovsky interested himself in the affairs of his village as if he had been a patriarchal landowner. He noticed that the peasant children ran wild and free at all hours of the day, getting into mischief, learning nothing but idleness and viciousness. Inquiry revealed that there was no school for these children. At this time there was no such thing as a public school in Russia, of course; private schools were provided for the sons and daughters of the well-to-do, but nothing whatever was provided for the peasant children. Should a beast of burden be taught to read and write? Thus the government reasoned.

Tolstoi had taken a radical step when he opened a free school on his estate, and himself taught the children of the serfs. Tchaikovsky decided that he could do no less for Maidanovo. He went to the priest of the local church. Would the church provide teachers and a place to hold the school if Tchaikovsky found the money for it? The church would. Tchaikovsky furnished the money out of his own income. Even so, the permission of the government had to be obtained. In due course of time, permission arrived. Tchaikovsky put on his long fur coat and round fur cap and plowed energetically through the January snow to attend the opening of his project.

This interest in the village welfare led to one piece of folly. It was the composer's habit to walk for two hours every day. In summer, the children met him at every turn of woodland path or road and begged him for kopeks. The more kopeks that were forthcoming, the more the news spread and the more children who appeared to beg. Tchaikovsky's friends were amazed and heartily amused one day to find the composer hiding like a thief under a small bridge in the effort to escape a mob of children searching for the giver of kopeks.

Gardening became a hobby with the composer, who planted all kinds of seeds and then lay awake nights for fear the frost would kill his early plants. His diary, somewhat neglected before, began to assume bulky form. He filled it with observations on the village life, his garden, famous people, art, philosophy. Among the most interesting entries are his remarks on great composers.

Of Beethoven he wrote: ". . . Beethoven, whom I praise unconditionally, and to whom I bend as to a god. But what is Beethoven to me? I bow down before the grandeur of some of his creations, but I do not love Beethoven."

Of Mozart, he said: "To my mind, Mozart is the culminating point of all beauty in the sphere of music. He alone can make me weep and tremble with delight. . . . Beethoven makes me tremble too, but rather from a sense of fear and yearning anguish."

Concerning Brahms he wrote: ". . . Brahms is so chaotic, so dry and meaningless!"

In 1866, the composer made a trip through the Caucasian region to Tiflis, where brother Hippolite was living. The magnificent scenery of the Georgian region, where the post carriages were flanked by armed guards as protection against the fierce brigands from the hill *auli* (villages), made a profound impression.

Tiflis, with its Eastern look, delighted him. He wandered up and down winding streets bordered by blossoming fruit trees. He stood gazing with an artist's pleasure at the old Armenian churches and David's monastery on the hill. The composer painted a vivid picture of the trip in a letter to Modeste:

"Early on Sunday (30th) I started in a four-horse post carriage, accompanied by a guard, whose sole duty is to look after the requirements and comforts of the travelers. I had not slept the preceding night on account of the horrible bed and the insects (when I think of the *best* hotel in Vladikavkas I feel quite sick), and thought therefore that the beauties of the Georgian Road would make but little impression on me. The road is, however, so grand, so astonishingly beautiful, that I never thought of sleeping the whole day long. The variety of impressions did not allow my interest to flag for a moment. At first the approach to the mountains was slow, although they appeared to be quite close to us, and yet we still drove on and on. Then the valley of the Terek became narrower, and we reached the wild and gloomy Darjal Gorge. Afterwards we ascended into the region of snow. Shortly before I started on my journey there had been an avalanche, and hundreds of miserable-looking natives were busy shoveling away the snow. At last we were driving higher and higher between great snow walls, and it was necessary to put on our furs.

"By six o'clock we were descending into the Aragva Valley, and spent the night in Mlety. I occupied the *imperial rooms.* After the dirt of the Vladikavkas hotel I found the clean rooms, good beds, and daintily set table very delightful. I dined, took a little walk by moonlight in the gallery, and went to bed at nine o'clock.

"Next morning I started off again. Already we could feel the breath of the south in the air; the sides of the mountains were cultivated, and constantly there came in sight picturesque *auli* and all kinds of dwellings. The descent was made at a terrific pace, considering the curves of the road. Not far from Dushet such a wonderful view came in sight that I almost wept with delight. The further we descended, the more the influence of the south wind was felt. At last we reached Mtskhet (noted for the ruins of its castle and the celebrated cathedral), and at half-past five we reached Tiflis. Toly and his wife were not there; they had not expected me till later, and had gone to meet me at Mtskhet. They did not arrive till eight o'clock.

'Meanwhile I had had time to wash, dress, and see something of the town. It is delightful. The trees are not yet all green; the fruit trees are in full blossom; a mass of flowers in the gardens. It is as warm as in June—in a word, really spring—just as it was four years ago when we left Naples. The chief streets are very lively; splendid shops, and quite a European air. But when I came to the native quarters I found myself in entirely new surroundings. The streets mean and narrow, as in Venice; on both sides an endless row of small booths and all kinds of workshops, where the natives squat and work before the eyes of the passersby. . . .''

In 1888 Tchaikovsky had reached the peak of his fame. The hermit of Klin was persuaded to come out of his cave and consent to a tour of the European capitals. Before he made the final arrangement, however, he determined to conduct three concerts in Russia. He did not relish the idea of having stage fright before an audience in Paris or Berlin.

He made the experiment with his own opera, *Vakoula the Smith* (sometimes called *The Little Slippers*, sometimes *Les Caprices d'Oxane*). Before the first performance, he wrote confidently:

"If all goes well, I believe that not only will my nerves be none the worse, but it will have a beneficial effect on me."

This was mere whistling in the dark, however. After the performance he wrote:

"I did not expect to be very excited on the day of the performance, but when I awoke, quite early, I felt really ill, and could only think of the approaching ordeal as of a horrible nightmare. . . . Consequently, at the appointed hour, I appeared half dead at the theater."

His heart fluttered like a moth and his mouth was dry as parchment as the composer took up the baton on that first evening. It took courage to go through the ordeal. Tchaikovsky, who did not believe in defeat, found that courage. News of his niece Tatiana, who had dropped dead at a masked ball, reached him the following morning. It took more than ordinary courage to go through with the next two performances, but the composer did this also. The third attempt at conducting convinced him that he would not disgrace himself if he accepted the tempting offers to conduct his works abroad.

Accordingly in 1888 he set out for Leipzig, where he was to meet his agent and make final arrangements for an extended tour.

As at Maidanovo, he kept a diary. These pages were filled not with school projects and other village affairs, but with descriptions of brilliant banquets and receptions, of huge concert halls where the finest orchestras performed Tchaikovsky's works under the baton of the composer.

The pages bristle with famous names: Scharwenka and Artôt (Désirée had grown fat and out of voice, but was as charming as ever); Wolf, Bülow, Dvořák; Brodsky, Siloti, Brahms, and Grieg, who met together at a New Year's Dinner. Tchaikovsky and Grieg were fast friends from this time on. The sad-eyed Russian, who had admired the Norwegian's music for many years, found the composer even more to his liking, fell in love with Nina Grieg's singing, later dedicated the *Hamlet* overture to Edvard Grieg.

The climax of his tour was the amazing festival held in his honor in Prague. The Czechs of Bohemia are a Slav people, and, as Modeste wrote: "There is no country in which music is better loved, or more widely understood, than in Bohemia. Nor is there any other nation which feels such appreciation for all that is Russian; not merely as a matter of passing fashion, but on account of actual kinship between the Eastern and Western Slav."

Tchaikovsky was made blissfully happy by the ten-day celebration. "It pleased him," said Modeste, "that Prague—the first place to recognize the genius of Mozart—should pay him honor, thus uniting his fate with that of the illustrious German."

Snow is on Kaz - bek, for - ev - er there in slum - ber

21

After Tchaikovsky returned from his tour in 1888 to the quiet of his little home, he wore his fame for the world to see; but he carried concealed the wounds of the struggle that had preceded that fame. An old Caucasian song runs—

> Snow is on Kazbek, forever there in slumber;
> There, too, in slumber a daring warrior lies;
> A gentle soul, he perished of wounds long ago.

Such a gentle warrior was Peter Ilich, who had gone forth to battle against the difficulties of life with poor weapons and no shield to cover him. Rising superior to all his weaknesses and trouble, he had won the right to say that he had created well and sincerely, that he had been true to himself.

Only five years were left for Peter Ilich. In that five years, however, he worked as he never had worked before. In spite of his traveling—another tour of the Continent, a visit to faraway America, a trip to England to receive the Cambridge degree of Doctor of Music—he found time to write music. Five great works are a monument to his industry.

The *Sleeping Beauty Ballet* and the *Casse-Noisette Ballet*, from which he prepared the famous *Nutcracker Suite*, are two of the most charming ballets ever written. *Sleeping Beauty* is built around the well-known fairy tale of the princess fated to prick her finger with a rose thorn and fall asleep for a hundred years, not to be awakened until a prince brave enough to enter the enchanted castle kisses her.

Tchaikovsky's music for this charming tale is right out of fairyland. It takes us to the enchanted castle, where even the flies on the wall fell asleep and the horses in the stables stood motionless when the spell was upon them.

Tchaikovsky, who loved waltzes and never missed a chance to use them in every work that would permit, has given us a charming bit of three-four rhythm in *The Sleeping Beauty*.

A character dance which depicts the feline movements of the booted cat and the white cat is a masterpiece of musical suggestion. We hear the meowing of the cats, almost see their fawning advances and lightning-quick withdrawals.

The Nutcracker Suite and the ballet from which it was taken were based on the German tale by Hoffmann. The story goes that a little girl, Claire, receives instead of a doll or other toy a nutcracker for Christmas. It is in the form of a droll little man whose jaws open and shut. The child is bitterly disappointed at such a hopelessly unromantic gift as an ordinary household nutcracker and leaves it downstairs when she goes

Waltz from "Sleeping Beauty"

The Sleeping Beauty—Waltz

Waltz from "Sleeping Beauty"

The Sleeping Beauty—Waltz

to bed. Late at night, however, she decides to steal down and have a look at the funny little man. On the stairs she is overtaken by a large number of mice. The nutcracker, seeing the child's distress, comes to life and leads the lead soldiers belonging to the boys of the household in battle against the Mouse King. The mice get the better of the battle until Claire kills the Mouse King with her slipper. At that point, the nutcracker changes into a handsome prince, who flies with Claire to the Kingdom of the Sugarplum Fairy, somewhere in Araby. There the toys and the sweetmeats join in a frolic to celebrate the romance of the little girl and her Prince Charming.

The *Overture Miniature* has a dainty, almost Mozartian theme. Above and below this theme flute notes dart like bright hummingbirds, and the short piece is closed by soft notes of the celesta, an instrument then new to the orchestra, one which Tchaikovsky had heard for the first time as he strolled through an obscure little street in Paris. (Below on the left.)

The *Marche* (above on the right) is bright and strutting, with pompous brasses leading the way, followed by the somber basses and the hurrying scales of the deep-toned strings. Clashing cymbals bring up the rear.

The *Dance of the Sugarplum Fairy* is dainty and rather languorous. The celesta, the clarinet, and the plucked strings interpret this dance. (See the top of page 14.)

The *Trepak* is distinctly Russian music. It is the sort of vigorous stamping dance which the composer saw the Cossacks or the peasants on Prince Galitsin's estate perform. Strings, trombones, and wild wayward tambourines, and finally the full orchestra, play for the dancers. (Below, left.)

The *Arab Dance* (above on the right) is a plaintive Eastern air, sung by the muted strings and woodwinds, with now and then a fragmentary melody from the oboe, the English horn, and the bass clarinet. Lightly now and again the tambourine tinkles, like the bangles on a Moslem girl's ankle.

The *Chinese Dance* is frolicsome and noisy. Droning bassoons, snapping notes plucked from the violins, shrill cries from the flute, quick calls of the woodwinds, bell-like notes from the glockenspiel—these make a good-natured tumult.

The *Dance of the Mirlitons* employs the flutes to suggest the toy instrument the *mirliton*, which produces a sound not unlike that made by means of a comb with tissue paper wrapped around it.

The *Waltz of the Flowers* sweeps gracefully along with woodwind, harp, horns, and strings.

The *Queen of Spades*, an opera with a dark plot taken from Pushkin's work of the same name, contains much music descriptive of the sinister theme of death and madness. Here, as in many others of his operas, Tchaikovsky was handicapped by choice of subject. Though he often expressed the desire to have a story about real people, whose emotions he understood, he more often than not had to work with an unreal plot, dealing with hideous and morbid subjects.

The *Queen of Spades* has in it some reality, despite its fantastic plot. For that reason, this opera, together with *Eugene Oniegin*, is still played today, mainly in the Soviet Union.

After his second tour of the Continent, in 1889, Tchaikovsky went again to Tiflis to visit brother Hippolite. During this visit he received alarming news. A letter from Nadejda von Meck informed him that her fortune was seriously curtailed, that she would have to stop his pension.

Loss of the money was no great matter to the composer, who by this time could live very comfortably on what his music made for him. He hastened to assure Nadejda that he understood, that he wished to help her in his turn. He was deeply wounded when the request came from her not to continue their correspondence. The whole thing was coldly done —in a way which could not fail to cut Tchaikovsky's proud spirit to the quick.

Then, when he learned that the widow was as wealthy as ever, he was stunned. Why had she acted in this way? If she did not want to continue the pension, the kind thing would have been to give an honest reason, not try to deceive him with a story which even a child would not believe. His every attempt to penetrate the mystery failed. To the end of his days he carried the wound of this unfriendly act.

The truth was, Nadejda was very ill. Certain family troubles had developed, too. She knew that the composer had enough money to live on. She reasoned that it would be wicked of her to spend precious time away from her own problems to carry on correspondence with this man she had not cared to speak to. Thus Nadejda undid much of the good she had done.

To this period belongs the Fifth Symphony, which carries forward the idea of an unfriendly force hampering mankind. The theme that embodies the fate idea is contained in the first movement, and is carried clear through the symphony to the finale.

From the Fifth Symphony

A short opera *Iolanthe* was begun just before the composer went to America. The "Romanze" from this work is nostalgic, delicately melancholy music in twelve-eight time.

Carnegie Hall was to be opened in New York, and Walter Damrosch, wanting a prominent composer as guest artist for the occasion, decided upon Tchaikovsky. The offer was too attractive to refuse, though the Russian composer started on the long ocean voyage with dread. The leavetaking was not happy in any sense; for the day before he sailed, he received the news that his beloved sister Sasha had died. Tchaikovsky had no heart for foreign travel and new laurels after that news, but an engagement had been made and Tchaikovsky the true professional did not fall down on his contracts. He did not speak of his great grief, but his eyes were sadder than usual during the voyage, and the famous people who entertained him in New York were baffled in their efforts to make him happy.

The huge brick building with its terra-cotta enrichments, its groups of polished pilasters of Peterhead granite, and elaborate bronze lanterns and wreaths was alive with people on the festival opening night of May 5th. Tchaikovsky made his appearance on that night, directing his *Marche Solennelle*. Standing straight and slender before the large orchestra, with every seat in the auditorium filled with hushed, expectant listeners, he raised his baton confidently. What would Laroche or Kashkin have said then of the panic-stricken young conductor they had known, the one who became ill with fright and feared that his head would fly off? That one surely had gone forever, and in his place stood an assured artist, one who had climbed the heights and stood there calmly proud of his achievements.

The *Marche* was enthusiastically received, as were the Third Suite, played on May 7th, and the two *a capella* choruses performed on May 8th. The composer was wined and dined by everyone who could get to him with an invitation. Among these were Andrew Carnegie, who astonished Tchaikovsky by his resemblance to the dramatist Ostrovsky and his power of mimicry. For the composer's amusement, Carnegie gave an imitation of Tchaikovsky on the conductor's podium.

It was with a sense of relief that Tchaikovsky slipped quietly from the city where the buildings were actually thirteen stories high (so he had written in a letter home), where multimillionaires played clown for their guests, where everyone ate mammoth dinners (so it seemed to him, who congratulated his cook on meager meals), where the newspaper reporters gave a visitor no peace.

Back home again in Klin he began to compose his greatest symphony, his Sixth, named the *Pathétique* by brother Modeste.

The solo bassoon utters the introductory phrases, the most despairing Tchaikovsky ever penned.

This utterly melancholy theme is taken up by the strings, the cellos and basses making an almost intolerable keening in the background against violas and violins as the introduction ends and the first movement begins.

Woodwinds and strings seize upon the theme of woe and terror, protesting, denying the assertions of the ominous phrases. As if weary of the struggle, however, the orchestra subsides into the sighing of the thin upper tones of violas, and there is a pause.

The tragic mood is tempered somewhat when the violins,

muted, voice assurance that there is hope, after all. The cellos join in this comforting melody.

This hopeful melody sings its way sweetly and with a sort of resigned melancholy, rising briefly to a vehement climax, quickly subsiding as if weary, also, of the struggle. The last four notes are murmured in the low range of the bassoons.

Suddenly a discord, crashing from the whole orchestra, destroys the brief dream of peace and hope. Tremendous screaming chords pour resistlessly from the orchestra. It is a giant crying out against fate. The music is fierce, terrible in its protest. Then the opening theme of despair returns, rages through the orchestra. Woodwinds and strings shriek defiance. Sonorous basses intone the somber Russian Liturgy for the Dead.

The struggle subsides. There are tender passages, memories of happier times, of loved ones lost. The strings *pizzicato* move softly downward, and above them the brass voices a noble, deeply moving phrase.

The second movement is in five-four time, a waltz which is not a waltz. There is an effort to be gay, but above the limping waltz rhythm the low-pitched melody moving in the cellos and woodwinds against *pizzicato* strings is tinged with pathos.

A second theme contains in it the memory of tragedy.

In the third movement, the orchestra rouses itself, "takes up arms against a sea of troubles," asserts a determination to vanquish the theme of defeat and despair. The oboe sounds the call to battle.

The fourth movement is grief and heartbreak. It is the lamentation of a soul crying out against fate. Fate, nevertheless, is stronger and overwhelms the protests and denials. Death, stronger than life, has conquered. This movement is a requiem, an expression of bitter and inconsolable grief.

Tchaikovsky went to St. Petersburg to conduct the first performance of the *Pathétique*. The most melancholy of symphonies was received with a sort of bewildered uneasiness by the audience. It was neither a failure nor a success. Tchaikovsky seemed not to mind.

Modeste and the friends with whom he spent the next few days noticed nothing unusual in the composer's manner. They were quite unprepared for his sudden illness. Horror overcame them when the doctors announced that the composer was dying of cholera.

Suffering from the agonizing cholera cramps, Tchaikovsky said over and over, "I believe this is death."

Noticing that his favorite nephew Bob Davydov was present in the sick-room, he smiled a shamefaced, wan smile, and said, "You will lose respect for your old uncle, seeing him in such a state."

At the very last, he repeated one name, mournfully and reproachfully. That name was *Nadejda*. At three o'clock on the morning of November 6th, he roused from delirium. His eyes, those sad eyes which seldom lighted with a smile, tried to do so for the sake of the watchers by his bedside. Then with a tired sigh, Peter Ilich Tchaikovsky slipped away from his troubled world, where he had won his stormy victories.

Finale

Faithful Alexis Safronov grieved over the death of the composer as sincerely as any of Tchaikovsky's relatives did. With his own savings he bought the house at Klin and gave orders that nothing was to be moved or changed about in the rooms. Pictures, piano, tables, chairs—these were to be left "as the master wished them."

Modeste gave a hand too, and between them they managed to gather music manuscripts, letters, cigar-holders, pens, and reading glasses—anything that remained of Peter Ilich Tchaikovsky's possessions. Then they opened the house as a museum. After the Revolution, the Soviet Government added more material to the collection and established Yuri Davydov, Tchaikovsky's nephew, as curator.

Upstairs, Tchaikovsky's private apartments have been preserved just as they were when the composer wrapped up the score of his Sixth Symphony and left for St. Petersburg. On the desk in the living-room are thirty cigar-holders of every kind, many of them works of art with carvings and incrustations; a medicinal pencil with which Tchaikovsky rubbed his temples when he had headaches; his pince-nez; a writing pad with some names and addresses scrawled out; a tuning fork and key for tuning the piano.

The piano holds the place of honor, just as it did when the composer lived, in the middle of the room. This piano was never tuned by the composer—he, of the sensitive ear, declared that it never lost its tune.

Bookcases with works of Pushkin, Shakespeare, Byron, Flaubert, Rousseau, Lucretius, Spinoza, Schiller, and Gogol.

A collection of batons; one, decorated with silver, had once belonged to Mendelssohn, who gave it to his friend Adolf Henselt, who in turn gave it to Tchaikovsky.

The bedroom contains a small bed with a curiously hideous drapery on the wall at the head, and a picture called *Melancholy* on the wall above it. This painting of the sea at night, with an eerie moon beginning to appear from behind dark ominous clouds, was a present from an unknown woman in Germany. The composer never parted with the strange picture, taking it with him even on his travels.

Tables of all shapes and sizes and plain chairs drawn up before them have been left as they were scattered by the composer through the rooms. On the plain little table in the bedroom the *Pathétique* was written.

Below, a small garden, where Tchaikovsky puttered among his flowers. Beyond, highways and truck gardens growing vegetables for Moscow, and the little groves where Tchaikovsky hunted his beloved mushrooms.

On the door of the house, a card left by the composer: *Not at Home—Please Do Not Ring.*

A modern Soviet writer, K. Grigorovich, visiting the museum before the Russo-German War, was reminded of the castle of the *Sleeping Beauty Ballet*. "All life is suspended," he wrote, "waiting to be released from the charm. Who knows but that the master may enter, alive as his compositions, seat himself at the piano and bring the house to life with his harmonies and melodies?"

NOTE:—In the summer of 1941 the Nazi troops, invading Russia, attacked Klin and did great damage to the Tchaikovsky house—how much, it is as yet impossible to say. Some of the manuscripts and furnishings were carried to safety by the curators, and—according to report—these were replaced when the town was later retaken by the Russians. The exact extent of the loss and damage, however, cannot be ascertained until the war is over.

Acknowledgments

The author's appreciation and thanks are hereby conveyed to the following persons and organizations for help and advice which facilitated the gathering of material for this book:

1. The American-Russian Institute, 101 Post Street, San Francisco, California: Miss Rose Isaak, Secretary.
2. Mr. M. Moukasey, Secretary of the Vice Consulate USSR, Los Angeles, California.
3. Mrs. Elizabeth C. Moore, author of *An Almanac for Music-Lovers*, who read and criticized the book in manuscript.

Quotations from *The Life and Letters of Peter Ilich Tchaikovsky* are reprinted by permission of the publishers, Dodd, Mead & Company.

The poems *Chaos*, by Krylov, and *The Cup of Life*, by Pushkin, are reprinted from Champney's *Romance of Russia*, courtesy of G. P. Putnam's Sons.

Music of *Marche Slave*, by Tchaikovsky, is included as it appears in the publication of Edwin H. Morris & Company, New York, N. Y.

All excerpts from Tchaikovsky's music, with the exception of *Marche Slave*, were taken from the thematic catalog of Tchaikovsky's works (*Catalogue thématique des œuvres de P. Tschaikowsky*) by permission of the Am-Rus Music Corporation, New York, N. Y., publishers and exclusive distributors of the catalog in the United States.

Brief excerpts from the following Russian folk-songs were taken from *Sixty Russian Folk-Songs*, compiled by Kurt Schindler, reprinted by permission of the publisher: Copyright, 1918, 1919, by G. Schirmer, Inc., New York, N. Y.

From Volume I—*Postilion's Song; The Slain Cossack; Riddle Song; Down on Mother Volga; The Bells of Novgorod; The Legend of Young Nightingale; Dobrynia Bids His Mother Farewell; The Feast of Vladimir; The Girl Who Would Not Dance; Vanya; The Wedding Suit.*

From Volume II—*Volga Boat-Song; The Beggar's Blessing; The Birchwood Splinter; The White Snow; Advice to Lovers; The Sowing of the Millet.*

Excerpts from the Russian folk-songs *The Birch Tree, Yuletide,* and *The Bending Branch* were taken from the *Botsford Collection of Folk Songs*, compiled and edited by Florence Hudson Botsford, reprinted by permission of the publisher: Copyright 1922, 1930, by G. Schirmer, Inc., New York, N. Y.

Excerpts from the following Russian folk-songs are reprinted by permission of the Belmont Music Company, Chicago, Illinois, from their publication *Russian Songs:*

Stormy Breezes; One, Two, Three; Ey Dubinushka (Song of the Toiler); *Troika; Kazbeck.*

Bibliography

The Life and Letters of Peter Ilich Tchaikovsky, by Modeste Tchaikovsky, edited by Rosa Newmarch. London and New York, John Lane, 1906; New York, Dodd, Mead & Company, 1924.

Tchaikovsky, His Life and Works, by Rosa Newmarch. New York, Charles Scribner's Sons, 1908.

P. I. Chaikovsky, Life and Work, by B. Yarustovsky. Centenary Edition, Moscow, 1940.

Tchaikovsky, by Edwin Evans. New York, E. P. Dutton & Co., 1906.

Tschaikowsky, by Ivan Otto Knorr. Berlin, "Harmonie" (publishing society), 1900.

Tchaikovsky, by E. Markham Lee. New York, Brentano's, 1904.

"Beloved Friend," by Catherine Drinker Bowen and Barbara von Meck. New York, Random House, 1937.

A Day with Tchaikovsky, by May Byron. (Days with the Composers series.) London, Hodder & Stoughton.

Tschaikovsky, by Richard H. Stein. Stuttgart, 1927.

Mezzotints in Modern Music, by James Huneker. New York, Charles Scribner's Sons, 1920.

From Grieg to Brahms, by Daniel Gregory Mason. New York, The Macmillan Company, 1902.

Musicians of Sorrow and Romance, by Frederic Lawrence. London, C. H. Kelly, 1913.

Famous Composers, by Nathan Haskell Dole. New York, Thomas Y. Crowell Company, 1937.

Catalogue thématique des œuvres de P. Tschaïkowsky, edited by B. Jurgenson. New York, Am-Rus Music Corporation, 1942.

P. I. Chaikovsky: Symphonic Music, by A. Budyakovsky. Leningrad, 1935.

Chaikovsky as a Symphony Composer. Press Department publication of VOKS (Society for Cultural Relations with Foreign Countries), 1940.

> Note.—Information on VOKS publications, as well as on the Centenary Edition mentioned below, may be obtained from the American-Russian Institute, 56 West 45th Street, New York City.

The Story of One Hundred Symphonic Favorites, by Paul Grabbe. New York, Grosset & Dunlap, 1940.

Stories of Symphonic Music, by Lawrence Gilman. New York, Harper & Brothers, 1907.

"Tchaikovsky's Second Symphony, a Neglected Masterwork," by S. Barnett, in *Musician*, May 1940.

"Tchaikovsky's Sixth Symphony," in F. Young, *Mastersingers*. Philadelphia, J. B. Lippincott Company, 1906.

The Pianoforte Works of P. Chaikovsky. Press Department publication of VOKS, 1940.

"It Will Never Be So Good: Piano Concerto in B flat minor," by G. R. Marek, in *Good Housekeeping*, October 1941.

"Master Lesson upon Canzonetta from the Concerto" (B flat minor), in *Etude*, June 1940.

Forty Songs by Peter Ilyitch Tchaikovsky, edited by James Huneker. Boston, Oliver Ditson Company, 1912.

Chaikovsky and the Theatre. Centenary Edition. Moscow-Leningrad, 1940.

Stories from the Operas, by G. Davidson. Philadelphia, J. B. Lippincott Company, 1931.

The Book of the Opera and the Ballet, and History of the Opera, by Frederick H. Martens. New York, Carl Fischer, 1925.

* * *

New Outline History of Europe, 1815-1940, by Henry Wilson Littlefield. New York, Barnes & Noble, 1940.

Story of Nations, by Lester B. Rogers, Fay Adams, and Walker Brown. New York, Henry Holt & Company, 1934.

Russia of To-day and Yesterday, by Nevin O. Winter. Boston, L. C. Page & Company, 1929.

Romance of Russia, by Elizabeth W. Champney and Frère Champney. New York, G. P. Putnam's Sons, 1921.

Russian Literature, by Avrahm Yarmolinsky. Chicago, American Library Association, 1931.

The Works of Alexander Pushkin, edited by Avrahm Yarmolinsky. New York, Random House, 1936.

A History of Russian Music, by M. Montagu-Nathan. London, William Reeves, 1928.

History of Russian Music (Vol. II), compiled by A. Groman, D. Zhitomirsky, U. Keldish, and M. Pekelis. Moscow-Leningrad, 1940.

Manners and Customs of Mankind, edited by John Alexander Hammerston. New York, Wm. H. Wise, 1937.

The Book of Festivals, by Dorothy Gladys Spicer. New York, Womans Press, 1937.

Tales of a Russian Grandmother, by Frances Carpenter. New York, Doubleday, Doran & Company, 1933.

The House That Music Built: Carnegie Hall, by Ethel Peyser. New York, Robert M. McBride & Company, 1936.

*   *   *

The International Cyclopedia of Music and Musicians, edited by Oscar Thompson. New York, Dodd, Mead & Company, 1939. Article on Tchaikovsky by Daniel Gregory Mason.

An Almanac for Music-Lovers, by Elizabeth C. Moore. New York, Henry Holt & Company, 1940.

The Listener's History of Music (Vol. II), by Percy A. Scholes. New York, Oxford University Press, 1930.

*   *   *

Soviet Music, Chaikovsky issue, 1940.

"Chaikovsky," by Reinhold M. Glière; "The Home of a Great Artist" (Klin), by D. Dubrovsky; "The Favorite of Millions," by K. Grigorovich—articles in *Sovietland*, April-May 1940.

P. I. Chaikovsky, a Brief Biography. Press Department publication of VOKS, 1940.

Chaikovsky's Last Home (The House-Museum at Klin). Press Department publication of VOKS, 1940.

"Mikhail Yrevich Lermontov," in *The American Review on the Soviet Union*, October-November 1941.

"Chaikovsky," in *Theatre*, May 1940.

"Further Light on Tchaikovsky," by N. Slonimsky, in *Musical Quarterly*, April 1938.

"The Truth about the Mysterious Death of Tchaikovsky," by S. Bertenson, in *Etude*, June 1940.

Biographical sketch in *Etude*, November 1937.

"Music at Home," by G. R. Marek, in *Good Housekeeping*, September 1940.

"Tchaikovsky on Broadway," by G. R. Marek, in *Good Housekeeping*, April 1941.

"Peter Ilyich Tchaikovsky," by M. Fisher, in *19th Century*, August 1940.

"Pathétique; Story of Genius," by Olin Downes, in *New York Times Magazine*, May 5, 1940.

"W.P.A. performs Tchaikovsky with 16 rifles and a 10-gauge gun," in *Newsweek*, August 8, 1936.

"Tchaikovsky in English—Philadelphia Opera Company," in *Newsweek*, November 11, 1940.

"Portrait" in *Time*, October 23, 1939.

Tchaikovsky's Works

FOR ORCHESTRA

Opus 13 Symphony No. 1 in G minor (*Winter Dreams*) (1868)
Opus 15 *Festival Overture on the Danish Hymn* (1866)
Opus 17 Symphony No. 2 in C minor (*Little Russian*) (1873)
Opus 18 *The Tempest*, symphonic fantasy (1873)
Opus 29 Symphony No. 3 in D major (*Polish*) (1875)
Opus 31 *Marche Slave* (1876)
Opus 32 *Francesca da Rimini*, symphonic fantasy (1876)
Opus 36 Symphony No. 4 in F minor (1877)
Opus 43 Suite No. 1 (1879)
Opus 45 *Capriccio Italien* (1880)
Opus 48 Serenade for String Orchestra (1880)
Opus 49 *Festival Overture "1812"* (1880)
Opus 53 Suite No. 2 (1883)
Opus 55 Suite No. 3 (1884)
Opus 58 *Manfred Symphony* (1885)
Opus 61 Suite No. 4, *Mozartiana* (1887)
Opus 64 Symphony No. 5 in E minor (1888)
Opus 67a *Hamlet*, fantasy-overture (1888) [See Incidental Music, Opus 67b]
Opus 71a Suite from *Casse-Noisette* (The Nutcracker Suite) (1892) [See Ballets, Opus 71]
Opus 74 Symphony No. 6 in B minor (*Pathétique*) (1893)
Opus 76 Overture, *The Storm* (1865)
Opus 77 *Fatum*, symphonic poem (1896)
Opus 78 *The Voivoda*, symphonic ballad (1897)

Without Opus Number:
>   Overture in C minor (unpublished) (1865)
>   Fantasy-Overture, *Romeo and Juliet* (1870)
>   *Elegy* for strings, in memory of Samarin (1884)
>   Coronation March (1883)
>   *Solemn March* (1885)
>   Military March (1893)

CONCERTOS

Opus 23   Piano Concerto No. 1 in B flat minor (1874)
Opus 26   *Sérénade mélancolique* for violin (1875)
Opus 33   *Variations on a Rococo Theme for Cello* (1878)
Opus 34   *Valse-Scherzo*, for violin (1878)
Opus 35   Violin Concerto in D major (1878)
Opus 44   Piano Concerto No. 2 in G major (1880)
Opus 56   *Concert Fantasy*, for piano (1884)
Opus 62   *Pezzo Capriccioso*, for cello (1887)
Opus 75   Piano Concerto No. 3 in E flat (1894)
Opus 79   *Andante* and *Finale*, for piano and orchestra (post-humous)

OPERAS

Opus 3   The Voivoda (1868):
>   (1) Overture
>   (2) *Entr'acte* and *Air de ballet*
Opus 14   Vakula the Smith (also called Little Slippers or Les Caprices d'Oxane) (1874)
Opus 24   *Eugene Oniegin* (1878)
Opus 68   *Pique Dame* (*The Queen of Spades*) (1890)
Opus 69   *Iolanthe* (1891)
Without Opus Number:
>   *The Oprichnik* (1872)
>   *Joan of Arc* (1879)
>   Mazeppa (1883)
>   *The Enchantress* (1887)

INCIDENTAL MUSIC

Opus 12   *Snegourotchka (Snow-White)* (1873)
Opus 67b *Hamlet*, sixteen incidental numbers [See For Orchestra, Opus 67a]

BALLETS

Opus 20   *The Swan Lake* (1876)
Opus 66   *The Sleeping Beauty* (1889)
Opus 71   *Casse-Noisette* (1892) [See For Orchestra, Opus 71a *(Nutcracker Suite)*]

CHAMBER MUSIC

Opus 11   String Quartet No. 1 in D major (1872)
Opus 22   String Quartet No. 2 in F major (1874)
Opus 30   String Quartet No. 3 in E flat minor (1876)
Opus 42   *Souvenir d'un lieu cher*, for violin and piano (1879):
        (1) *Méditation*
        (2) *Scherzo*
        (3) *Mélodie*
Opus 50   Trio in A minor, for violin, cello, and piano, "In memory of a great musician" (Nicholas Rubinstein) (1882)
Opus 70   *Souvenir de Florence*, string sextet (1892)

PIANO MUSIC

Opus 1   Two Pieces (1867):
        (1) *Scherzo à la russe*
        (2) *Impromptu*
Opus 2   *Souvenir de Hapsal* (1867):
        (1) *The Ruined Castle*
        (2) *Scherzo*
        (3) *Chant sans paroles*
Opus 4   *Valse caprice* (1868)
Opus 5   Romance in F minor (1868)

Opus 7 Valse-Scherzo in A major (1870)
Opus 8 Capriccio in G flat major (1870)
Opus 9 Three Pieces (1871):
          (1) Rêverie
          (2) Polka de salon
          (3) Mazurka de salon
Opus 10 Two Pieces (1871):
          (1) Nocturne
          (2) Humoresque
Opus 19 Six Pieces (1874):
          (1) Rêverie du soir
          (2) Scherzo humoristique
          (3) Feuillet d'album
          (4) Nocturne
          (5) Capriccioso
          (6) Thème original et variations
Opus 21 Six Pieces on One Theme (1873):
          (1) Prelude
          (2) Fugue
          (3) Impromptu
          (4) Funeral March
          (5) Mazurka
          (6) Scherzo
Opus 37 Sonata in G major (1879)
Opus 37a The Seasons, twelve characteristic pieces, one for each
          month (1876)
Opus 39 Children's Album, twenty-four pieces (1878)
Opus 40 Twelve Pieces (1878):
          (1) Etude
          (2) Chanson triste
          (3) Funeral March
          (4) Mazurka
          (5) Mazurka
          (6) Chant sans paroles
          (7) In the Village
          (8) Valse
          (9) Valse
          (10) Russian Dance

(11) Scherzo
(12) Réverie interrompue
Opus 51   Six Pieces (1882):
(1) Valse de salon
(2) Polka peu dansante
(3) Menuetto scherzoso
(4) Natha-Valse
(5) Romance
(6) Valse sentimentale
Opus 59   Dumka (1886)
Opus 72   Eighteen Pieces (1893):
(1) Impromptu
(2) Berceuse
(3) Tendres reproches
(4) Danse caracteristique
(5) Méditation
(6) Mazurka pour danser
(7) Polacca de concert
(8) Dialogue
(9) Un poco di Schumann
(10) Scherzo-Fantasie
(11) Valse Bluette
(12) L'Espiégle
(13) Echo rustique
(14) Chant élégiaque
(15) Un poco di Chopin
(16) Valse à cinq temps
(17) Passé lointain
(18) Scène dansante
Without Opus Number:
Sonata in C sharp minor (posthumous)
Fifty Russian Folk Songs, piano duet (1868)
Weber's *Perpetual Motion* transcribed for left hand
alone (1873)
Impromptu-Caprice for piano, dedicated to Mme.
Sophie Jurgenson (1885)
Valse-Scherzo for piano (posthumous)
Impromptu for piano (published in the *Book of the*

Old *Students of the Conservatory*, dedicated to
Anton Rubinstein) (1889)
Impromptu for piano (posthumous)

SONGS

Opus 6   Six Songs (1869):
               (1) *Heed Not*
               (2) *A Summer Love Tale*
               (3) *What Torment, What Rapture!*
               (4) *A Heavy Tear*
               (5) *Why?*
               (6) *None But the Lonely Heart*
Opus 16   Six Songs (1873):
               (1) *Berceuse*
               (2) *Attends!*
               (3) *This Only Once*
               (4) *The Song That You Sang Long Ago*
               (5) *What Matters?*
               (6) *Chanson grecque*
Opus 25   Six Songs (1875):
               (1) *The Sleep of Sorrow*
               (2) *Comme sur la cendre encore chaude*
               (3) *Chanson de Mignon ("Kennst du das Land")*
               (4) *The Canary*
               (5) *Je ne lui ai jamais parlé*
               (6) *The Czar's Drinking House*
Opus 27   Six Songs (1875):
               (1) *Invocation to Sleep*
               (2) *Clouds*
               (3) *O, Never Leave Me, Sweet Friend*
               (4) *Le soir*
               (5) *Dès le jour qui me naître*
               (6) *A Love Pæan*
Opus 28   Six Songs (1875):
               (1) *No, Whom I Love I Will Not Name*
               (2) *Les Corails*
               (3) *Vision*

(4) No, I Have Never Loved
(5) No Tidings Came From Thee
(6) Sweet Maid, Give Answer

Opus 38 Six Songs (1878):
(1) Don Juan's Serenade
(2) The Dawn of Spring
(3) The Tapers Were Flashing
(4) Oh, If You Only Would
(5) L'Amour d'un mort
(6) Pimpinella

Opus 47 Seven Songs (1881):
(1) Had I Known
(2) Unsatisfied
(3) Le Soir et le matin
(4) The Sounds of Day Are Still
(5) To the Forest
(6) Only for Thee
(7) J'étais une petite herbe

Opus 54 Sixteen Songs for Children (1883):
(1) Grandmother and Grandson
(2) The Little Bird
(3) Spring
(4) My Garden
(5) Legend
(6) At the Seashore
(7) Winter Evening
(8) The Cuckoo
(9) Spring
(10) Cradle Song During a Storm
(11) The Floweret
(12) Winter
(13) Spring Song
(14) Autumn
(15) The Swallow
(16) Lullaby

Opus 57 Six Songs (1884):
(1) Tell Me
(2) Remorse

(3) *Oh, Do Not Ask*
(4) *Go To Sleep*
(5) *Consolation*
(6) *Only You*

Opus 60   Twelve Songs (1886):
(1) *Last Night*
(2) *Verschwiegenheit*
(3) *O, wüsstest du*
(4) *The Nightingale*
(5) *Simple Words*
(6) *Sleepless Nights*
(7) *Gypsy Song*
(8) *Adieu*
(9) *The Night*
(10) *Die Lockung*
(11) *Courage*
(12) *Starry Night*

Opus 63   Six Songs (1887):
(1) *Do You Remember?*
(2) *At the Open Window*
(3) *You Do Not Love Me*
(4) *The First Meeting*
(5) *A Night in July*
(6) *A Serenade*

Opus 65   Six French Songs (1888):
(1) *Serenade*
(2) *A Broken Tryst*
(3) *Waiting*
(4) *Let Winter Come*
(5) *Tears*
(6) *A Little Witch*

Opus 73   Six Songs (1893):
(1) *By the Drowsy River*
(2) *Night*
(3) *Moonlight Night*
(4) *When the Sun Goes Down*
(5) *Melancholy*
(6) *Weil ich wie einstmals allein*

Without Opus Number:
> Four Songs (1873):
>> *Emporte mon cœur*
>> *Les yeux bleus du printemps*
>> *Je voudrais mettre dans une seule parole*
>> *Nous ne nous promenerons plus longtemps*
>> *Schnell vergessen!* (1870)

VOCAL COMPOSITIONS FOR TWO OR MORE VOICES

Opus 41   *Liturgy of St. John Chrysostom* (Russian Mass, a cappella) (1878)

Opus 46   Six Duets (1881):
> (1) *Le Soir*
> (2) *Ballade écossaise*
> (3) *Tears*
> (4) *In the Garden by the Brook*
> (5) *La passion finie*
> (6) *Sunrise*

Opus 52   *Russian Vesper Service,* choral work (1882)

Without Opus Number:
> *Romeo and Juliet,* duo for soprano and tenor (posthumous)
> *Homage to Anton Rubinstein,* choral work (1889)
> *Night,* vocal quartet (adapted from Mozart's Fantasy No. 4 for piano) (1893)
> *Nature and Love,* part song (1871)
> *Ten Russian Hymns* (liturgical choruses, including *Hymn to Saint Cyril and Methodius*) (1885)
> *Moscow Cantata* (for the coronation of Alexander III) (1883)
> *Schiller's Ode to Joy Cantata* (manuscript) (1865)
> *Cantata for the Polytechnic Exposition* (manuscript) (1871)
> Chorus, dedicated to the students of the University of Moscow (1889)
> Chorus, dedicated to the Imperial Opera of St. Petersburg (1889)

GENERAL INDEX